ONE FROM EACH COLUMN

ONE FROM EACH COLUMN

My 46-Year Trek from Abusive Childhood to Elusive Motherhood

Jodi Mitchel Tolman

Published by Game Changer Publishing

Paperback ISBN: 978-1-967424-01-6

Hardcover ISBN: 978-1-968250-02-7

Digital ISBN: 978-1-967424-03-0

www.GameChangerPublishing.com

*To my three remarkable, loving, and supremely supportive children,
without whom there would simply be no story to tell.*

*And to my husband... my brass ring. I truly don't know
where I'd be without you.*

ACKNOWLEDGMENTS

I must first thank Helane Siegle Staller, who declared, "That's amazing! You should write a book and call it "ONE FROM EACH COLUMN!" upon learning that I was pregnant and would soon have one genetic child, one adopted child, and one born from a donor egg. It took twenty-six years to write, but Helane lit the fire!

My former neighbor and fellow author Kendra Vaughan Hovey goaded me into writing after notifying me that if I didn't write my story, she would. She asked, "What're you going to do for the rest of your life? Sit in a chair?"

My dear friend Barbara Wall Lobosco, who named Fightin' Little Jodi one summer day on her deck, and whose unflagging encouragement made me believe that I could write this book.

My wonderful friend, Shari Lobe, who, after reading the first few chapters, imbued me with confidence when she emailed the magic words... *"OH HONEY, YOU'RE A WRITER!"*

My sweet friend, Karen Lacks, always asking for more as she read bits and pieces, and whose steadfast belief in me resulted in a book with more than six chapters.

My college buddy and dear friend, Donald Heymann—writer, editor, coach, and adjunct professor at NYU—for his loving support and generous first edit. His email saying, *"You've got something here, Jode,"* meant more than he could ever know.

To my high school classmate, Brad Graham—Nicky Arnstein to my Fanny Brice in our senior class production of *Funny Girl*—now co-owner of Politics & Prose, DC's premier indie bookstore, my great thanks for his faith in my incarnation as an author.

My new and trusted friend and author/editor, Lynne Feldman, whose expertise gently guided me, and helped shape the narrative in ways I could not have accomplished.

My powerhouse friend, Marci Bracken, co-publisher of *Pink Chair Storytellers*, whose offer to feature my story in her groundbreaking magazine for women is profoundly appreciated.

To my brilliant and gifted therapist, Christine Shruhan, who for sixteen years has tenderly and skillfully guided me to mental and emotional health. You have my undying gratitude.

To all those and so many more, I offer my deepest and heartfelt thanks.

ONE FROM EACH COLUMN

My 46-Year Trek from Abusive Childhood
to Elusive Motherhood

Jodi Mitchel Tolman

PREFACE

Countless books have been written about overcoming adversity. Myriad self-help tomes are out there on becoming a stronger and more resilient person in the face of great obstacles and even trauma. Volumes exist on traversing the landscape of infertility. Innumerable treatises can be found on parenting and the skills required to raise independent, confident, healthy children. And much has been written on what constitutes and creates a loving bond between parent and child.

One From Each Column aims to encompass all of the above, but with one overarching goal: providing some perspective and guidance to those facing infertility—be it primary, secondary, or age-related—and perhaps fretfully considering options. Assisted reproductive technologies? Adoption? Donor? Surrogacy? Or perhaps, dear reader, you're contemplating the painful possibility of abandoning altogether your dream of becoming a parent.

The burning questions underlying these agonizing considerations are almost always the same, questions my husband and I have been asked umpteen times.

- Will I be able to love a child brought into my life through alternate methods with the same depth and dimension as a child I would bring into the world "naturally?"

- Will that child bond with and love me as deeply?
- What if I already have a child, but cannot conceive again?
- What if I adopt a second child or have another through surrogacy? Will that child occupy the same place in my heart as my biological child?
- Will these children feel differently about one another than had they been conceived by the same method?

These sometimes confounding and always profound questions are the reason I put pen to paper, and it is my fervent hope that in these pages can be found inspiration, encouragement, optimism and promise.

I invite you on my arduous—and ultimately triumphant—journey over many years and myriad challenges, from childhood abuse to building my family through alternative methods. Perhaps you will see yourself along the way. I hope you enjoy the ride!

CONTENTS

INTRODUCTION

I figure if you're going to dream, you don't fuck around. Otherwise, why bother? I have fiercely yearned for many things throughout my life. To grow up in a functional family, escape a punishing household, gain approval from a disparaging father, have a sprawling family of my own, and ultimately live a life in service of humanity.

To give you a sense of how impossibly wide the span of my pipe dreams was, here are a few examples of what was included on the list. At eleven, I asked my mom if Jewish girls could become nuns. Lovingly repressing a guffaw, she said perhaps and wondered why I asked. Because nuns live the most selfless lives. (I have always been an absolutist, frustrated in the gray, which can be challenging for the mere mortal. If you're going to devote yourself to service, it doesn't count unless you're all in, I figured, like Mother Teresa.) My aspirations toward the nunnery dissipated by eleven and a half, replaced by other ambitions, among them an Academy/Grammy/Emmy/Tony Award-winning career in music and acting, romance beyond reason, and morphing into famed zoologist Jane Goodall.

As a maximalist in all things, I find the notion "less is more" annoying. Math tells us less is never more. More is more. I believe in more cheesecake, more justice, more laughing off of asses, more dogs, more art, righteous indignation, kindness, chocolate, raging against authority, hummingbirds, world travel, jewelry, empathy, good stand-up comics, butterflies, adventure and activism, for a start.

I developed a desire for romantic love at a young age. As I reached my early twenties and realized that fertility is finite, a fabulous relationship producing a bunch of gorgeous kids topped the wish list, now longer than a CVS receipt. By then, love and kids came first. Lots of kids. It turned out, however, that the road to even my humble dreamscape was littered with signposts flashing sneering skepticism that these wishes would ever come true.

But I wasn't about to ride off into the sunset resigned to childlessness. Resignation was never my strong suit. A tough upbringing in an abusive household forced me to forge the steel of resilience, resolve, and perseverance in the fire of trauma and pain. I wasn't Superwoman, but I did become my own Fairy Godmother. And with repeated waves of what often felt like a three-thousand-pound wand, my sweetest dreams came to life.

That's what happens when a forty-year-old woman with ferocious determination gets up, dusts herself off after squandering her fertility across two failed marriages, and bangs her iron will against a ruthless biology.

My daunting but ultimately triumphant journey led me from abject misery at thirty-three, when a dangerous first marriage ended in divorce, to my third and thus-far-final marriage at nearly forty to Mr. Right. At forty-six, that bunch of kids I'd hoped for so long was in the building. What I couldn't know was that my "bunch" would include three children, each arriving via a different mode of transport—one "natural," one adopted, and one from a donor egg. I still wonder how the hell I pulled it off.

I came out on the other side with profound gratitude, and I share my story hoping it might uplift and inspire those facing infertility. I want you to know, my dear reader, that with hope comes the promise of triumph—always—and answers you're yearning to hear.

But let me start with *The Decision*—one that defined my life in more ways than I could've known, ultimately setting me on the path, albeit a circuitous and sometimes treacherous one, to prove those signposts wrong.

CHAPTER 1
WELL, *THAT* WAS SETTLED

It was October 1978. I was in my huge, nearly empty apartment at Riverside Drive and 92nd St. on the Upper West Side of Manhattan. I'm sure there were stunning apartments in the pre-World War II building, but mine wasn't one of them. Earlier that evening, I sat in the middle of the cavernous living room with a long-ago-elegant parquet floor, now tired enough to make you weep. A rickety card table and two flimsy folding chairs sat *waaay* across the room from a small TV. And I mean small. Squinting to see the screen, I hoped it was Paul Newman I was watching. I was always hoping it was Paul Newman.

You might think that living in this austere aesthetic would be depressing. It wasn't depression. It was indifference, which demands much less interest and discipline than decorating. Plus, I had more important things to ruminate on than sofas and area rugs.

I now sat cross-legged on my bed, chin in hand, pondering a consequential and weighty question I'd been mulling over for a very long time. The room was silent, save for the sound of the steady rhythm of my slow and deep breathing—and cars and trucks, annoyingly audible from my first-floor digs.

I sat for quite some time in this room absent another stick of furniture, where crumpled bed sheets stood in for curtains. They were ill-equipped to keep out the morning sun, but it didn't much matter since I'd jerry-rigged a sleep mask out of a navy blue knee sock left over from my aspiring preppie days at the age of twelve, enabling me to sleep 'til noon on a regular basis.

I had a choice to make, and that evening—in that dimly lit room, smelling not-so-faintly of the then wildly popular Opium cologne wafting from every piece of clothing I owned—I made it.

If by the time I turned twenty-eight, I had not fallen in love with a sperm donor in the shape of a good-looking, delicious, brilliant, hilariously funny romantic who wanted nothing more than for me to be the mother of his children, I would hightail it to the nearest sperm bank and fall in love with a good-looking vial. I had no idea if my career as an actor would materialize, nor a clue about what a single facet of my life would look like, but this much I knew... I didn't suffer the trauma of abuse and emerge equipped with an unflinching determination to have kids for nothing. I would be a single mom if it came to it, and gather me a gaggle one way or another.

So there it was. *The Decision.* And twenty-eight was light years away...

...I was twenty-six.

Little did I know I'd be haunted by the same damn dilemma multiple times between twenty-eight and forty-five. My work was cut out for me. I just hadn't read the job description.

CHAPTER 2
A RUDE AND STAGGERING AWAKENING

I t was May 2012, as I sat in the cozy comfort and safety of my therapist's office in the same spot I always did when seeking her unerring guidance as I worked through a particularly confounding problem: the corner of the sofa, with the ever-present box of tissues at the ready on the side table. Christine always sat across the small room in her wing-backed chair with her feet resting on a small, upholstered footstool and a white-noise machine on the floor in the corner. I found this sameness from visit to visit soothing and somehow promising. She had the kindest face, and colossal strength to keep from internalizing the pain pouring from the hearts and heads of client after client in that room, day in and day out. Perhaps it was the yellow legal pad in her lap that captured the agony and kept her safe and sane.

It was here, on that lovely day in May, that Christine first spoke the word. *Abuse.*

What?? Did she say... abuse? The words I'd always used to describe the household that I grew up in were crazy, insane, volatile, scary, loud, violent... but never abusive. As my capacity to see and hear rapidly diminished, my heart raced, and slight nausea set in, and I struggled to absorb the blow. I was sixty, for fuck's sake, and this was the first time anyone had used that word to describe my dad's behavior when we were kids.

And in the midst of what felt like a death spiral came the most massive and slowest-moving epiphany in tsunami clothing I ever experienced. Ohhhh... so *that's* what it was. Yeah. That seems right. Well, I guess I've got the gist of it now. And I guess I've got some work to do.

Then, the memories came flooding in.

One late afternoon, when I was twelve and my brother Ira was fifteen, I stood nailed to the living room floor, frozen solid. The scream I was straining to unleash was tethered to my throat. Not even the desperate guttural utterances in my chest could come out. So with no ability to move or be heard, I had no way to stop my dad from dragging Ira up the steps by his hair.

Ira didn't make a sound that I recall but held onto my dad's arm with all his might—presumably in a frantic effort to lessen the pain and, I suppose, to keep his hair. About halfway up, my father either let go or lost his grip. Perhaps the creeping shame from the realization of what he was doing pried his hand open. Ira didn't utter a syllable. No expression of rage. No tears. He just passed my dad on the stairs and went to his room. Not a word was ever spoken about the incident.

And here's the truly mystifying thing—to this day, with quiet vehemence, my brother adamantly disavows the notion that our dad was abusive. My recollection of that horror is cinematic. Ira's is nonexistent.

My brother Gershon and I agree about our dad, although our recollections of so many things are vastly different. He saw my mom as the instigator. I saw her as my savior.

When I simply could not wrap my head around the fact that my brothers' perceptions of our upbringing could be so wildly disparate from my own, Christine, in her steady brilliance, explained, "You all had hold of the same elephant, but one held the trunk, one the tail, and the other the ear." I came to understand what had long been deeply perplexing—same elephant, divergent experience.

So, this accounting is my own. It comes from my memory alone. I speak for neither of my brothers, but from my vantage point, after eighteen years in that house. Additionally, I am acutely aware that, comparatively speaking, I had it pretty easy. For one thing, thank heavens, there was no sexual abuse. It was psychological and emotional, including intimidation, and the threat of, and on occasion, actual violence.

There were countless childhoods infinitely more harrowing than mine, which makes me feel a bit sheepish to be painting a picture of parental abuse. Nonetheless, that was my experience, and I share my story, in part, with the hope that others who may have had a similar upbringing—and perhaps are still suffering its effects—find encouragement in knowing that healing is possible. A life of emotional and psychological stability and fulfillment can be built. Most important is knowing that the abused need not, by default, become the abuser.

CHAPTER 3
SHIT STARTS TO HAPPEN

I honestly don't know what lit the fire in my belly to want children so badly. It could have simply been that I loved kids. Maybe it was my hope to one day recreate with my own daughter the adoring relationship I cherished with my mom throughout my life. Or perhaps it was the need to build a healthy, happy family to replace the painful dysfunction of my childhood.

Contradictory and mystifying dynamics in my parents' complex marriage, often simultaneously in play, made it impossible to understand what was truly going on at any given moment. There was compelling and observable evidence of their love and even adoration for one another. And screaming. *Lots* of screaming.

In an oft-repeated scene, my parents would be in the kitchen, locked in a ferocious battle over something or other. It always seemed to be about one of us kids, which meant it was somehow our fault, so less bearable than had it been about nothing of consequence.

In our cheerful '60s-style kitchen with avocado-colored appliances and Formica, playful wallpaper sporting large graphic flowers in greens, oranges, browns, and yellows, including on the ceiling, and a yellow linoleum floor, they stood yelling at each other. I don't know that either ever heard the other. They were spitting furious, with red faces, glazed eyes, and rigid bodies. That's when I retreated under the dining room hutch, desperate to escape to safety, if not quiet. I could fit because I was so small, but mostly because I clutched my knees with all my might and squeezed my body into a tiny ball of terrified little girl.

Burying my ears and face in my arms, with my eyes tightly shut, I would wait out the storm. It was somehow comforting, because there was so little space under there, and it felt like just about as much as I could manage.

I sat there for what seemed an eternity, with two distinct thoughts repeating on an endless loop as fear gave way to fury.

Don't they know I'm gone? And if they know, why aren't they looking for me? I'm just a little girl, for Chrissakes.

Their little girl. And I'm missing. The rage was vastly preferable to the fear. It didn't take me long to understand that one would empower me and the other could cripple me.

So my fury was born at an early age. As I grew, my dad's wrath honed in me a finely-tuned sense of outrage and rebellion, equipping me with the wherewithal to face and overcome, I believed, any obstacle. To be fair, I'm pretty sure I was enraged from birth, if not before. I'm preternaturally impatient. Hell, I can barely wait for the light to change. So it might've really pissed me off that gestation took nine freaking months. No doubt I felt ready at conception. Maybe my fate was sealed when born of the loins of the most tightly wound man who ever drew breath through clenched teeth. Who the hell knows?

But a never-predictable, sometimes dangerous, belittling environment hardly helped soften the edges. A disrespectful tone or the expression of a differing opinion, or a roll of the eyes so far back in my head it looked like I was having a seizure, or too loud a tsk, or too little reading, or too much eating, or a B instead of an A, or some imperceptible infraction got me screamed at, smacked, threatened with the belt, repeatedly grounded, and made to know I was a constant disappointment.

According to my dad, girls were considerably less than. Girls didn't do this, that, or the other thing. Included in the list was participating in those few-and-far-between delicious moments of fun, like wrestling with my dad in the living room on Sunday mornings. He and my brothers would be tangled up so tightly on the floor you couldn't tell whose arms belonged to whom and which legs were attached to whose body. Squeals of laughter laced with disbelief that my dad was in such a good mood impelled me to jump on top of the pile.

My father had a laugh like no other. Hearing it made me deliriously happy, especially as it was not often that I did. His laugh was ridiculously high-pitched. And he had a way of inhaling while laughing that launched the decibels even higher. It sent the entire family into gales of hysterics whenever we heard it, spinning shining golden moments of pure joy. It was in the midst of that sublime happiness that he would extricate himself from the heap, pluck me off the pile, and pitch me onto the couch. "Girls don't wrestle." Many sentences spoken in our household began with my dad insisting, "Girls don't..."

I was small to begin with, but being literally tossed aside, alone on the sofa while the three of them had the time of their lives, left me feeling even smaller. So small as to be invisible. Dismissed. Discarded. Unworthy. Of no value .

In between those moments of what seemed like happy-family normalcy, I railed against the rest, especially the incessant insistence that I want, do, think, and be something else. Something better. Something smarter. Something... *else.* The juxtaposition was stark—an impossible imbalance between joy and indignation, accompanied by the gnawing sense that I was not entitled to either.

My dad often insinuated that anyone who thought this or said that must be stupid. And I believed I was, well into adulthood. Still do in my low moments. But I certainly wasn't masochistic and realized there were times when, against every straining shred of my sanity, I had to acquiesce.

Living at the intersection of ire and submission was perplexing. My wrath often rescued me, but in the midst of my dad's tirades, occasionally and especially when violent, my heart broke for him. I hated him, yet could hardly stand it as I witnessed his system spew anguish, and his mind-boggling confusion as it dawned on him that he was not the dad he wanted to be. I knew in my shattered heart that he crossed a line he had not intended to but, in the frenzy of his fury, was unable to step back over. He was paralyzed, and the pathos was merciless. It slammed me in the solar plexus and grabbed me by the throat. I could barely breathe.

These were the moments when I swore to become a mother, determined to create an alternate scenario in the hope of building a counternarrative, desperate to undo the painful one I was living. My ironclad resolve to shield my kids from the fear, and confusion, and rage, and hatred, and shame, and loss, and guilt, and profound sadness that festered in me like a soul-devouring bacteria was born in these instants. I vowed to be the perfect mom. The only thing my children would know would be overflowing love, praise, pride, safety, stability, and self-worth that, even at my delicate age, I knew children deserved and needed to feel. It was then that I constructed my steely resolve to become a mother who would be loved, trusted, respected, and never ever pitied or, heaven forbid, feared.

What happened in my dad's life that broke him, I wonder, at least as a father? Quite successful in his professional and social life, he was well-respected and admired, a valued leader in our small community. Friends, colleagues, and neighbors would seek his advice and opinion. He was a treasured friend, being there whenever needed.

When our neighbor, Paul, one of my dad's closest friends, died of a massive heart attack in his fifties, leaving three young kids, my dad was available for his wife, Gerry. When my Uncle Normie, as he was affection-ately known, had a major stroke at forty-two, my dad helped Phyllis and her three kids through it. Norm was a strapping, sweet, and handsome guy whom we all adored, and severely debilitated for the remainder of his life, unable to speak intelligibly or walk. Until the day Norm died, my dad visited him every week, played cribbage with him, talked to him, listened to him, laughed with him, loved him. At home... it was something differ-ent. But the certainty I held so deep in my heart that my dad was a good and tender man enabled me to survive and come out the other side loving him.

My father's father emigrated from Romania and worked as a butcher in a local market. I have two distinct recollections of my grandfather. I remember him as a sullen, chain-smoking, unaffectionate, hard man with whom I had little engagement, who seemed intimidating and severely strict. I also have sadly few but cherished memories of sitting on his lap in his favorite chair in their small but always perfectly tidy one-bedroom apartment, where there was never a moment without the gorgeously deli-cious smells of my grandmother's Hungarian Jewish cooking drifting through the Old World air. Brisket. Stuffed cabbage. All manner of baked goods. Sheer scrumptiousness.

I was always mystified by the deep yellow stains on the first two fingers of my grandfather's right hand and his upper lip from years of smoking so heavily. I yearned to have a warm and loving relationship with my grandpa, and on occasion, I did.

I can't know what happened to my dad, but I recall an account that might shed light. The story has it that as a teenager, he came home late on one occasion from an evening with friends, which enraged my grandfather. As it was told, he forced my dad to stand for quite some time with his arms straight out to his sides, palms up—books stacked high on each hand.

Was my dad abused? Was he never good enough? Was he desperate for his father's love and approval, never receiving either in adequate measure? Was his fury born in those moments? I have no idea. But I certainly wouldn't be surprised.

Perhaps the greatest puzzlement in our immediate family is that there was never a word spoken amongst any of us in an effort to come to grips with my dad's behavior, and what, if anything, we could do about it. What saddens me so deeply still is none of us ever tried to help him. He was alone and ashamed in his abuse.

And where was my mom in all of this? The only time I remember her physically intervening involved a particularly angry altercation between my dad and Gershon.

My brother and I were in the kitchen when he asked me to deliver a letter the next day to the bartender at a cafe in the shopping district of Squirrel Hill, the Pittsburgh community where we lived. Sitting in his favorite chair in the living room, my dad would read everything he could get his hands on, but always with an eye and ear cocked so as not to miss any of us doing something we shouldn't. He was appalled to overhear Gershon ask his little sister to go into a bar.

As he made his way from the living room to the kitchen with startling urgency and temper observably rising, Gershon and I could feel the air grow heavy as the barometer dropped amidst the approaching menace. Whenever we saw our dad rip his reading glasses from his face in a lightning-quick gesture, we knew things were heading sideways. The decibels started to climb as my dad challenged Gershon. "How could you ask your fifteen-year-old sister to go into a bar?" Desperate to deescalate the tension with what he thought was humor and scrambling to brighten the gathering darkness, Gershon said, "I'm not asking her to turn a trick. I'm asking her to deliver a letter."

Now over the edge, pushed by Gershon's sarcasm and perceived insolence, my father lost all control. In a harrowing scene, the most violent since Ira was dragged up the stairs, my dad began to pummel Gershon, backing him up to the sink. My brother did not raise a hand in response, except as a shield. And I was once again paralyzed in horror. The moment was especially excruciating, as it somehow seemed to be my fault.

After what felt like forever, I was able to move and frantically attempted to get my mom to rescue my brother. She was upstairs in the shower. Not wanting to leave Gershon alone with my father, I stood at the bottom of the stairs in the front of the house screaming, "Mom! MOM!! You have to come down here NOW!!"

What's still incredible to me is with her very poor hearing, she heard me all the way in the back of the house over the noise of the shower. I screamed so loud I blew out my voice. Discovering when I tried to speak again that I couldn't was quite startling.

A visibly shaken, ashen Gershon had managed to make an end run around my dad and darted into the living room, seeking escape. My dad followed him, continuing to scream, when my mom, teeny tiny Paula Ruth, flew down the steps clad only in a towel and shower cap, dripping wet. She stood between my brother and dad, shrieking up into my father's face, "Roy! Roy! You're a maniac! Stop it!!"

Struggling to make his way back to some semblance of composure, he seemed to slowly return to reality. Defeated and distraught, he stood with his hands clenched in fists at his sides. In wretched misery, he repeated over and over, his tremulous voice losing strength with each repetition, "I'm your father. You can't talk to me like that. I'm your father. You can't talk to me like that."

It tore me apart. The despair in his hoarse voice, his bewilderment and indignity were unbearable. I wanted to rush to him, gather him up and fly away with him, rescue him. And the torment and embarrassment Gershon felt, especially in front of his little sister whom he knew adored him, made me want to save him, too.

But I was helpless, useless, and seemingly to blame. Feeling unutterable heartache for them both, I had a gut-deep desire to transform my dad into something he was not, but I believed he desperately wanted to be. It would turn out that my inclination to change men became a recurring theme throughout much of my adult life, leading me into less-than-healthy and sometimes dangerous relationships.

In the roiling sea of emotional chaos that was my family, I struggled to tread water. And I believed my mom was my life raft. She was the only source of comfort or quiet in my house and I honestly don't know what would have become of me without her. The dimension of our bond and depth of our mutual adoration meant everything to me from a very early age. She was my haven. My harbor. Safety. Stillness. Pure love. And hope.

There was a rocking chair in my small bedroom where she would hold me in her lap at bedtime when I was very young. She sang the same three songs to me every night in her beautiful, husky, soothing voice: "Stormy Weather," "Big Rock Candy Mountain," and "Summertime." Not only was the sound of her voice immensely calming, but its vibration as I rested my head against her chest was transcendental. It was as if she lulled me into a dream. Until I got too heavy, she was able to hold me in her arms as she rose from the rocker and put me into bed. Her ability to carry me across the room revealed her strength and made me know that even so small, she was mighty. And her might was not simply physical.

I somehow knew she had the power to withstand the winds that would buffet our family. I believed she would infuse me with that power and I'd be OK. She did, and I was. Later in life, I came to realize that strength was always within me, but it was my mom who gave it life, just as she had given me.

As I understood that little girls could grow up to become mothers, I knew in the deepest recesses of my being that I would. Fully aware that the profound connection to my mother would save me created a burning determination to one day build that bond with a daughter of my own. I believed my mom was my superhero protector, but as herculean as she was at five feet tall and one hundred ten pounds, she could not hold back the tide of my dad's temper. The little vessel that she was too often took on water, reminding me that even she couldn't keep me afloat.

Still, I managed to weather the storms, albeit battered. I certainly didn't emerge unscathed, but I didn't emerge a serial killer, either. My embattled psyche created a forceful coping mechanism in what would become my real superhero, reliably and repeatedly riding in to save the day.

Like the good-gal gunslinger emerging in slow motion from a cloud of dust, with the sun glinting off the sweat on her gorgeous brow, came

Fightin' Little Jodi—a short-for-her-age, skinny, scrappy kid in a dirty T-shirt and tiny torn jeans, with much of her kinky hair escaped from the failure of an inept hair band. Fightin' Little Jodi's default stance was with feet apart, chin jutted out, shoulders up to her ears, hands balled into fists on her nonexistent hips. Pissed off and hell-bent.

Fightin' Little Jodi and I waged war more times than I can recall, but the fiercest battle of all was figuring out how to gather that gaggle as I aged well beyond fertility. For now, suffice to say the calculation made on the bed in my Manhattan apartment was way off. Shit happened.

CHAPTER 4
ROY DAVID, MY DAD

Allow me to set the stage and introduce the supporting cast in the story. Getting to know and understand the players in any drama is always useful, ultimately enhancing the emotional payoff, whether it be devastating or uplifting. (I think it's safe to say you'll find plenty of both in these pages.)

My grandparents lost their first two children, each within a year of their birth. Such tragedy was nearly commonplace back then, but to overcome pain of that nature seems simply impossible. Somehow, they did, or tried to, and soon brought two more children into the world: Roy David and Violetmae. Perhaps the pain and anguish generated in my grandfather his own rage, rendering him broken and incapable of loving his surviving children wholeheartedly and unencumbered. Perhaps he resented them for surviving his first two cherished children. And who's to say whether that was internalized by Roy and Violet, causing their own self-doubt and the painful weight of survivor's guilt?

Maybe my grandfather succumbed to unfathomable depths of despair, questioning himself as a man and father, believing he was somehow to blame or wholly inadequate. Surely he could not have assuaged his wife's agony. And what lasting effect did facing a mother's greatest nightmare have on my grandma? The burden on their kids' emotional development had to have permanently impacted my dad and his sister. And yet, their parents functioned. They put one foot in front of the other and set about raising their surviving children.

Photos of my dad throughout his life revealed he was matinee-idol gorgeous. He was especially beautiful as a kid. Just a glance unveiled the truth... butter wouldn't melt in his mouth.

My grandfather's sister, my great Aunt Betty, was a fashion model in Manhattan in the 1930s and quite the looker herself. We have a photo of her demurely yet seductively peeking back over her bare shoulder with a rose in her teeth. She lived in Atlantic City and never married, but dated a string of high rollers and sported a gigantic diamond on her hand. Several snapshots in family albums show my dad sitting at Aunt Betty's knee in very expensive outfits, mostly sailor-themed, she had purchased for him. She doted on him—big time.

At one point, Aunt Betty asked my grandmother if she could adopt my dad, suggesting that since my grandma had two kids, she shouldn't mind parting with one. Apparently, she minded. Imagine that.

My Aunt Vi was also stunningly beautiful. Tall, alabaster-complected, and with jet-black hair, many said she looked like Hedy Lamarr. In fact, she went on to have two daughters and named the first Hedy.

I think my Aunt Vi added evidence to the possibility that my grandfather was abusive or, at least, exceedingly difficult to grow up with.

As a parent, she was much like my dad in temperament, but erratically irrational and compulsive, often very angry, strict, and demanding. Living in her house was also no day at the spa. I remember Hedy and her sister Nada, telling me how careful they and their dad needed to be when closing drawers in the kitchen. Aunt Vi could tell if they had been closed too fast, as the contents would be an inch or two from the front of the drawer. Drove her crazy.

She never sat with the family to enjoy a meal, but on a stool with her ever-present cigarette and ashtray (she eventually died of throat cancer), getting up to clear the table throughout the meal, washing dishes as the family ate. If anyone else smoked a cigarette in her house, she would follow them with an ashtray so that, God forbid, ashes would not fall on anything. My father also had an obsession with order. He was constantly squaring off objects on a table, or making sure nothing was out of place or alignment. I believe these traits in my aunt and dad stemmed from their all-encompassing need for control. As we know, few things in life are controllable, but those of us with Type AAA personalities struggle to control anything we can.

Despite the difficulties in my dad's household, listening to him talk about coming of age in Pittsburgh made it seem that he was a happy, well-liked kid. Some of my warmest and fondest memories of my dad were listening to him talk about his escapades. Not only were they fabulous stories, but they made me know in my heart that he had a fun, joyful childhood, at least in part. To be able to envision him in a carefree life meant much more to me than I knew at the time. As I aged, these memories became true treasures.

He loved to regale us with tales about his buddies and the trouble they got into. There was no such thing for me as hearing them too many times, and we heard them a *lot*. One of my absolute favorites is this...

When my dad was about fourteen, he and his buds stole a car one night from the lot of a rental place. Releasing the parking brake, they silently pushed the car off the lot, heading toward a hill to coast down. No running engine meant no headlights, of course, so my dad draped his body over one front fender, and another kid over the other, each holding flashlights, barely illuminating the way.

The flashlights now dead, they thought they heard something coming in the pitch darkness. Stopping within four feet of railroad tracks, they were able to see the train barreling down the line. Miraculously unharmed and thankfully undetected, they returned the car to the lot. My dad marveled at each telling that they avoided arrest and death on the same night.

Roy attended three different high schools in four years, but managed to have great friends and a solid social life. He dated quite a few girls, with stories to tell about each. His favorite was about his best friend, Izzy Stein, asking him to look after his girlfriend when he went off to the service. "Just take her out a few times, Roy," Izzy asked. Roy was happy to oblige.

My parents fell fast, but before long had to say goodbye as he went off to the Air Force to train as a radio operator. Stationed in Galveston, Texas, before deploying to Europe, he fell out of a plane on the tarmac and broke his elbow. It likely saved his life. My mom joined him in Galveston in 1945 along with their respective mothers, and they were married. Sadly, I know no details about their wedding. I know it was nothing fancy, as photos show my mom dressed in a stylish suit and my handsome dad in uniform.

Album after album painted an idyllic picture of a fabulous courtship, honeymoon in Colorado Springs, and an early life with wonderful friends. After the service, my dad was offered a job delivering Pepsi by his Aunt Dora's wealthy husband, Morris, who owned several Pepsi bottling plants in and around Ohio. Morris was more than wealthy. He was a wealthy asshole. My parents never forgave him as he refused to allow my dad to take time off to be with my mom at the birth of their firstborn.

Gershon was born in Mansfield, Ohio, and soon after, the family moved back to Pittsburgh. Both grandmothers wanted to have proximity to their first grandchild, and my mom didn't mind the idea of having some help with my brother while my dad worked several jobs to make ends meet. Five pregnancies, two miscarriages, and three kids later, our crazy family began to unfold.

It was then that my father's work ethic came into full view. Although he was eligible for the GI Bill that was available to returning veterans after World War II, he claimed to be unaware of the potentially life-changing benefit to which he was entitled. The bill would have enabled him to pursue higher education at no cost. He dreamed for many years of becoming a dentist, which could have been accomplished had he gone to college. Having only a high school education was one of several sources of his debilitating insecurity.

Not only did he have a dream of entering a profession, but he was also a lover of learning, constantly striving to know everything about anything that could be known, on any topic in any realm. Who knows what a college education would have meant in my dad's life, and what he might have achieved. As it was, with only a high school diploma to his credit, for many years he worked three jobs to support his growing family.

The work that became permanent was as a scrap metal broker for Tube City Iron and Metal, a small, family-owned company, buying and selling scrap metal to and from the mills, foundries, and scrap yards. Working at Tube City for nearly forty years, my dad built an admirable reputation in Pittsburgh as a highly respected broker who could be trusted, and with whom people in the industry were honored to work. Still, his reputation didn't confer the elusive attribute of self-respect. I believe it was from that empty well that emerged his greatest difficulties in life.

Despite the ever-rippling ramifications of my dad's self-doubt and deprecation, and the developing picture of their difficult marriage and our troubled household, one fact was abundantly clear—my parents were madly in love.

After many years of financial struggle, they managed to put a little money away for a small remodel of our living and dining rooms. This included installing a stereo system with speakers built into the walls. It was such a modest remodel, but it seemed extravagant.

Both were music lovers. A fabulous singer, my mom collected albums from the era's leading female vocalists—Ella Fitzgerald, Sarah Vaughan, Eydie Gormé. While I loved much of the music of my time, I couldn't get enough of the music my parents loved, which shaped my style as a performer later in life.

And they loved to dance. With the stereo installed, my mom and dad would head into the living room every night after dinner and dance to their song, "Twilight Time." They were wonderful dancers. While they danced, I would sit curled up on the velour sofa in our newly remodeled living room, complete with a beautiful tapestry of a New York City night-time street scene hanging on the wall across from the couch, hugging my knees to my chest. In those delicious moments of tranquility and joy, watching them float across the floor with beatific expressions on their faces, I couldn't imagine two people more in love. Life seemed to be nothing but perfect. And everything else faded away into nonexistence.

Many years later, I found a small metal box my mother had given me long ago that I had tucked away. It was filled with love letters to my mom from my dad in the service. The many photo albums I still have filled with pictures of my dad during his time in the Air Force have generously bestowed upon me the ability to imagine in vivid detail my incredibly handsome father on his bunk in the barracks, pining away for my mom and penning his heartbreakingly wistful love letters. He called her Inches. The aching tenderness of his love filled page after page of onion skin stationery, forming the foundation upon which their marriage was built and would be sustained through many challenges and much anguish.

Witnessing their ardor filled me with a deep desire to have exactly that one day. Unfortunately, experiencing the fallout from the dysfunction of their relationship, I assumed even the most loving marriage came with vitriol and ugliness. As the pain long percolating in our family rose to and breached the surface, it would be the depth of their love that would ultimately eclipse the heartache.

CHAPTER 5
PAULA RUTH, MY MOM

My mom grew up in a colorful household. And the color preceded her. When her grandfather died, leaving her grandmother to raise six young kids on her own, she earned a living extending credit to the local hookers, charging them interest on their loans. It wasn't exactly the House of the Rising Sun, but a house in a barely better neighborhood.

Not surprising that half the kids chose to live life on the slightly seamier side. Augusta, known as Gussie, grew up and married Morey Fox, who rubbed elbows in Miami Beach with the Jewish mafia. Their daughter, Roslyn, remembered being on the boardwalk as a little girl with her parents and their friends, sitting on the laps of uncles Bugsy (Siegel) and Meyer (Lansky).

My mom's uncles, William and Lou Gold, became small-time racketeers in Pittsburgh. William, known as Toughy, fixed tickets and who knows what else. Lou ran numbers. He actually acquired a bit of fame in Pittsburgh as a champion Golden Gloves welterweight boxer in 1912 and 1913, fighting under the name Young Goldie. A cherished artifact in our family is a promotional photo of Young Goldie in the ring, surrounded by men on bleachers, every single one of whom hid his face from the camera behind his Panama Boater.

From a very early age, my mom was impishly mischievous. In a photo of her at age five, she posed with her head slightly bowed, her nearly black eyes tilted up to the camera. A whisper of a smile made her look like Lucifer's Little Lovely. And her dad, whom she idolized, was equally devilish.

Plotting to ride the same bus one morning, purposely getting on at different stops, Mom saved the seat beside her for her dad to occupy when he boarded. They behaved like strangers. Striking up a conversation in voices loud enough for everyone to hear, they asked one another about their families.

My mother said, "We live on Monitor Street."

My grandfather replied, "We live on Monitor Street, too."

When he asked her name, she responded, "Paula Ruth."

He declared, "I have a daughter with the same name!"

When asked if she had siblings, she answered, "Yes, I have two brothers and a sister," then recited their names.

He exclaimed, "No kidding? Those are the names of my kids!"

At that point, my mother cried, "You must be my father!"

And my grandfather bellowed, "You must be my daughter!"

Then they got up and off the bus. Kills me.

Two years separated each child in my mother's family. Jerry came first, followed by Frank, then Edna Belle—who was called "Sister" when she was little, soon shortened to "Sis"—and finally, my mom, completing the quartet. My mom and Aunt Sis were very close, but certainly not without their sibling squabbles, each headstrong.

One episode occurred when my Aunt Sis appeared in the living room wearing my mom's favorite sweater. Objecting to her clothing being pilfered, especially her prized sweater, my aunt offered to return it immediately. My mom said she would appreciate that. "Shall I take it off right now?" My mom said she wished she would. Aunt Sis ripped open the sweater—shooting buttons off in every direction like tiny, round, but lethal projectiles (a miracle no one lost an eye!), destroying every button hole—then silently took it off and handed it back. I can only imagine my mother's reaction. On the flipside, they were loving sisters with many stories to tell of having the best times together. They liked nothing more than making the other roar with laughter.

My grandparents raised four children during the Great Depression.

How my grandfather kept the family afloat was a mystery. They moved many times—exactly how many is unknown—a few under cover of darkness when they were unable to pay the rent. It was never clear what my grandfather did for work. Sometimes he was a jeweler. Sometimes an optometrist.

Legend has it that he'd position himself at the train station at the end of the workday as hundreds of people disembarked. He'd set up a small stand with a sign that said Free Eye Exams. The tabletop was covered with a piece of black velvet, while hidden on a shelf underneath was a small dish of egg whites. A customer would approach for an exam, during which my grandfather would ever-so-lightly rub his finger along their bottom lid, surreptitiously dip it in the egg whites, then wipe it off on the black velvet, leaving what looked like a small bit of film. He would announce that he'd just removed a cataract. *That'll be three bucks.*

Family lore recounts my grandmother carrying a platter full of food from the kitchen to the dining room table, tripping over the dog on her way, and landing along with dinner on the floor. Her husband and four kids were all seated at the table when my grandfather, seriously annoyed that Jeff had the temerity to get under my grandmother's feet, flung his fork at the dog, which stuck in his side. With my grandmother still on the floor, covered with food, the kids rushed to Jeff to make sure he was unhurt. My grandfather exclaimed, "Of course! See to it that the dog's OK, but whatever you do, don't check on your mother!" Given that he made this exclamation while still seated at the table, it's fair to wonder if the irony was lost on him.

A very talented singer, my mom performed with a big band in Pittsburgh. The band leader eventually went on to become hugely successful scoring films. Many encouraged her to head for New York or Hollywood to make a name for herself, but she could never bring herself to leave her family. Aunt Sis played the piano and sang, too, and they'd perform as often as they could, including at the Manor Theater in Squirrel Hill before the start of the movie so they could get in for free, avoiding the fifteen-cent admission. When anyone agreed to indulge them, they'd entertain with their rendition of "Little Grass Shack," a huge hit when they were young, complete with choreography. Their duet was a staple in the family, even as the cousins were growing up. They were actually fabulously talented performers.

Paula Ruth was hilariously funny and an accomplished prankster. Every once in a while, at the end of my school day, I'd find her standing on the sidewalk in front of the house in her muumuu with the loudest colors and craziest pattern, my brother's huge high-top Converse sneakers on the wrong feet, a gigantic floppy hat on her little head, a ridiculously enormous purse on her arm, and a front tooth blacked out with Black Jack chewing gum.

We walked to and from school, and many kids streamed past our house on their way home. She would stand on the sidewalk and, in a dead-on Goofy impersonation, ask kids if they'd seen me. A girl in school remarked with great empathy that it must be difficult to have my mom embarrass me so. I set her straight. My mother's wild humor and absence of care about what anyone thought of her made me adore her all the more, and want to be just like her when I grew up.

Later in his life, my folks took on the role of caretakers of my Uncle Lou. He lived in a small apartment above a bar, "the Saloon," as he called it, owned by a man my uncle knew only as Junior. Uncle Lou ran numbers on the side. I never knew on the side of what, exactly. He likely suffered from dementia, but the family always said he was punch drunk.

He'd hang out in the Saloon, have a few shots, and—thinking he heard someone call him a dirty Jew—wheel around and throw a punch. When one landed, the police were called. They'd cart him off and call my mother to meet him at the police station. One night, he was let out the back of the paddy wagon, as they were known in those days, surrounded by police officers much taller than him. Of course, this was no accomplishment as my uncle was seriously short. When he saw my mom, he exclaimed, "Polly Ruth! I can't figure out why I'm bein' pinched!" After one incident, it was decided he should be hospitalized for observation. My parents got him settled into his room.

Uncle Lou would never be caught without a tie. We were always impressed by his desire to look oh-so-natty, even when just drinking in the bar. As my mom gathered up his clothing in the hospital and a few of his things, the truth behind his ever-present ties was revealed.

She discovered his tie felt crunchy. It was stuffed halfway up with bits of paper where he'd scribbled numbers and names to deliver to the race-track or his bookie. She also found a note in his shirt pocket saying, "My name is Lou Gold. If anything happens to me, Junior did it."

The next day, when my mom visited, she noticed he was leaving ten cents on his food tray at every meal. Realizing he was leaving a tip, she explained that he was not in a hotel, but the hospital, to which he replied, "Polly, I gotta take care of the girls."

He was the last of the Damon Runyon characters. And so funny. Every Friday night, he'd come for dinner. For as long as he could manage it, he'd come by bus. If we happened to wander through the dining room on a Friday in the late afternoon and glance out the window at just the right moment, we'd see him walking up the sidewalk with his head of thick silver hair, baggy pants puddling at his shoes, white shirt, utilitarian tie, and an overcoat my dad had given him that was four sizes too big. He looked like an elderly cartoon character. As soon as he stepped foot in the house, he'd ask my dad, "Have you got a highball in your vest pocket?" My dad would escort him to a small closet in the dining room with a few bottles of liquor on the top shelf that no one in the house ever drank from. Ever. (We're Jewish. We ate.) He'd pour Uncle Lou a shot of Schnapps, which was all he needed.

My grandmother would make chicken soup every Friday for Shabbat dinner, which we'd enjoy in the dining room, complete with the good china, silver, and crystal, all set on a crisp white tablecloth. With the Shabbat candles warmly glowing in the middle of the table, we did our very best to maintain an appropriately serene mood—no easy feat for the Mitchel/Friedman bunch. Like clockwork, the peace was invariably pierced when Uncle Lou put ketchup in his soup, where my grandmother's glorious homemade matzo balls proudly bobbed. Righteously appalled, Nana admonished her brother for the culinary affront of ketchup in the matzo ball soup, and he begged her to just leave him the hell alone.

After dinner, Dad would take him home and as they were leaving, Uncle Lou and I would perform our little vaudeville act.

I'd say, "Bye, Uncle Lou!"
And he'd say, "See you Wednesday."
My response was always, "What's Wednesday?"
To which he'd answer, "I don't know, but be there early."

Uncle Lou never knew the name of a single one of his great nieces or nephews, calling all the girls "Mabel" and all the boys "Chief." And none of us could imagine our family without him. Sadly, our kids never knew Uncle Lou, but the middle name of Gershon's son, Josh, is Young Goldie.

My mom's life was not without heartache. Her dad died from a burst appendix just before Gershon, my grandparents' first grandchild, was born. Despite never knowing him, all thirteen of my first cousins and I felt his absence acutely growing up, as we'd been captivated by side-splitting stories about him and had a very good sense of what we were missing. Our four families were extraordinarily close, spending birthdays and celebrating holidays together, entertaining one another and performing whenever asked, or for no good reason. I recall having an appreciation throughout my childhood for the closeness of my mom's side of the family and the incredible fun we all had together, hoping it would never change.

Brains and humor were coveted commodities in the Friedman clan, and many of my cousins possessed both in spades, along with several of my aunts and uncles, not to mention my mom. Passover Seders were among the most enjoyable times we had as a family. As we cousins reached our teenage years, Seders grew to include twenty to thirty people as we began bringing friends and "sigos" (significant others).

My family always hosted the Passover Seder, but our house was so small, fitting everyone was a challenge. Family members alone numbered twenty-four. And as the kids got older, our numbers would swell, at which point, we had to hold our Seders at a local banquet hall.

Until then, we'd place several folding tables in a row perpendicular to the dining room table that stretched into the living room, with folding chairs rented from the local funeral home. Once everyone was seated, no one could get up unless they were near the heads of the tables. Each of the families brought food to share, and my Aunt Sis's husband, Uncle Bill, who grew up in an Orthodox home and was extremely observant throughout his entire life, led our Seders with deadly seriousness. Lasting nearly two hours, no food was served until the Seder concluded, other than bits of the ritual foods, and lots of wine—otherwise, not a bite.

My mom, in true rebel fashion, would invariably ask within seven minutes of the start of the Seder if it was time to eat. We were all expecting it, and as soon as she asked, we peeled off into hysterics. My Uncle Bill wanted to shoot her, but somehow got through the remainder of the service without committing homicide. Finally, it was time to eat, and dinner was positively raucous. Our Seders produced some of my most cherished family memories.

Paula Ruth had what was called a "fun wig." Popular at the time, these were worn by women who didn't need a wig. My mother's was short and dark, and looked much like her own hair. I could never figure out the point. One summer morning, driving to work in her wig (and I assume clothes, too), she stopped at a red light. A car full of teenage boys pulled up next to her, pointing and laughing with one another, and just generally behaving like obnoxious, stupid teenage boys.

While looking straight at them, she put her hand on top of her head and yanked off her wig. She looked completely bald as her hair was tucked under a tight-fitting, nude-colored stocking cap. The boys were horrified, not knowing what they were seeing. The light turned green, and she drove away. She always got the last word.

Mom worked in a retail shop "up street," as the shopping district in Squirrel Hill was called. We had no garage and when she left for work on this particular morning, her car was parked in front of my dad's on the side of the house. As it happened, he would be going to work late that morning. In the course of negotiating her departure from the parking spot, she backed into my dad's car, busting the driver's side headlight and doing some damage to the front fender. She needed to get to work, so she scribbled a note saying, *"I'm sorry I hurt your car,"* added our phone number, and secured it under the windshield wiper.

When my dad left the house, he noticed the damage. Incredibly irritated but not having time to deal with it as he had to get to work himself, he pulled the note off the windshield and, without reading it, stuffed it in his pocket. Sometime after getting to the office and completing his morning tasks, he turned his attention to the car, fishing the note out of his pocket. In the midst of making the call, he realized the number he was dialing was ours, unmasking the culprit.

The considerable irritation that had only grown since he left the house pretty much evaporated. It's hard to be mad at someone you love so much and think is so freaking funny. When my mom answered, he said, "This is Roy Mitchel. I'd like to talk to the person who hurt my car."

She said, "I'm sorry. You'll have to speak to my husband," and hung up.

I think he loved her a little more that day.

Periodically losing her voice and being instructed by her doctor not to whisper, as that could damage her vocal cords, my mom took to carrying a pen and pad of paper when voiceless. When I was fairly young, she had a case of total laryngitis. We were in the car going grocery shopping when a driver cut her off as we were about to pull into the parking lot of the Giant Eagle supermarket. My mother was incensed.

She flew into the lot and screeched into a space, jumped out of the car, leaving me in the front seat, and ran as fast as she could toward the offending driver. She not-so-lightly tapped him on the shoulder and when he turned around, silently but frantically wagged her finger in his face, miming that he better stay put while she scribbled a note.

I was watching the entire encounter and remember the incredulity on his face. She maniacally shoved the notepad up to his face so he could read the following: *"I have my small child in the car, you asshole, and you just cut us off! This is a citizen's arrest! Don't move! I'm going to find a police officer!!"* She ran into the market to find a cop. I'm sure you can figure out how long he waited for her to return.

Paula Ruth and I used to love to stay up very late, just the two of us, chatting about all kinds of things and laughing our heads off. Long after everyone had gone to bed, we'd sit in the small, matching occasional chairs on either side of the table lamp in the living room. The house was hushed, and with us seemingly alone in the world and no one to intrude on our reverie, we delighted in these special evenings together. She had a funny habit of timing things on the "upswing," just past the half-hour. Whether it was washing dishes, doing laundry, or making a phone call, she preferred to do it on the upswing, including heading up to bed after one of our epic nocturnal lovefests.

She wore a gold watch with a very small, gold-colored face and small, flat, rectangular-shaped gold clasp with the head of a long-horned steer stamped on it. One evening after we'd been chatting for hours, bleary-eyed and without her reading glasses, she glanced at the clasp of her watch, thinking she was looking at its face, and said with alarm, "Oh my God, Jodi! We have to go to bed! It's a quarter to three!!" It was 11:20. When we realized why she thought it was 2:45, we got uncontrollably hysterical. She peed in her pants.

Her irreverent humor and delight in shocking people remained undiminished her entire life. My dad, the consummate "always-be-prepared" Boy Scout, wanted to make their end-of-life preparations and felt they should visit the funeral home that would handle the arrangements when they passed away. Time to shop for caskets!

At the funeral home one afternoon, the young son of the director, just getting started in the family business, was carefully and with great sensitivity presenting the inventory in the showroom. In the understated elegance of the setting, with soft lighting and solemn music piped in, speaking in appropriately hushed tones, he pointed out the different features of each coffin.

"This one is mahogany with gleaming brass handles, and that one is solid oak with a white satin interior," he said.

Carefully inspecting each and comparing prices and styles, my mom took her time.

Seeming to have settled on one, she asked the young man if he had a step stool. He said he felt sure there must be one on the premises and respectfully asked why she wanted one, unable to imagine a single scenario in which she would need a step stool.

She said, "This one looks nice. I'd like to get in."

"You want to get into the casket?" he queried, with not a hint of blood left in his face.

She responded, "Well, of course. If I'm going to spend eternity in a box, I'd like to make sure it's comfortable."

My dad leapt to the rescue of the poor, shaken kid, assuring him my mom was kidding. Of course I can't know, but I'm guessing he didn't remain in the family business.

CHAPTER 6
GERSHON

Gershon was the first of sixteen kids between my parents and their four siblings. I have practically no recollection of him from when I was young other than in photos. My memories start when he was in high school and gorgeous. He was nicknamed "Lover Boy." Girls were all over the place, and my friends were crazy jealous that I got to live in the same house as Lover Boy. I was six years younger and madly in love with him.

I used to dream that any boyfriend I had or, better yet, husband I might land, would look exactly like him. I'm sure he went through that awful, awkward phase, but I never saw it. All I saw was an elegant kid resplendent in his khakis, perfectly pressed knock-off Brooks Brothers shirts, and shiny penny loafers, complete with gleaming pennies.

He wanted to be Johnny Mathis and would break into one or another of his biggest hits on a regular basis, always with one hand on his chest, where it rested through the entire song. He actually managed to sound something like him.

When he wasn't singing Mathis' greatest hits, he loved to sing "O Sole Mio," the operatic masterpiece, with his hand in its place. Of course, he could only sing the song's title and made up the rest of the Italian as he went along. It was hilarious.

And what a magnificent swimmer he was. He was captain of the swim team and our family never missed a meet. I was mesmerized watching him silently cut through the water with strength, speed, and grace, creating barely a ripple. His coach felt he had real potential and offered to train him for an Olympic trial, but asthma derailed that dream. I never knew what impact, if any, the disappointment had on him.

Sadly, we had no relationship that I can recall. Perhaps it's merely a memory failure, but I remember very little interaction and very few shared experiences.

But we did share the abuse, though we never sought refuge in one another. We suffered alone in our respective silos. Gershon and I were both outspoken when we could manage it, and as the oldest, he bore the brunt of our dad's fury until he moved out, when that distinction fell to me. We did share political proclivities, and I remember shouting matches with my dad around the dinner table as the Vietnam War raged before our very eyes on our TV, along with millions of families around the country. What an effective digestive aid. The nation was collectively insane.

There was a time when my big brother protected me from a potential threat. I cannot recall how old I was, but I was young. Playing a block away from the house on a beautiful sunny day in our perfectly safe little neighborhood, an older man approached me. I had never seen him before. He struck up a conversation, asking my name and where I lived. He seemed nice enough. I don't recall if I told him my last name or indicated where my house was.

He asked about my family and did I have any brothers or sisters. I offered that I had two older brothers. He then asked, "Do your brothers ever sit on top of you and shake?" I was instantly uncomfortable. However young I might have been, I was old enough to feel the inappropriateness of his question. I said my mother was waiting for me and I had to go home. I turned on my heel and ran all the way.

Gershon was in the kitchen, and I told him what had happened. My mom was on the phone for what was likely to be a lengthy conversation—it was always a lengthy conversation—in a tiny room off the hall between the kitchen and dining room that we called the Little Room. It was stuffed with books and the Encyclopedia Britannica, papers and pens and pencils, and a small aquarium. My mom sat at a little counter where the phone sat, with a notepad she had stapled together from scraps of paper, which she liked to doodle on while chatting with friends.

Gershon interrupted her, which we were never permitted to do unless someone was bleeding or a life was about to end. And it couldn't be just any life. It had to be the life of one of us. (My mom remembered one time when Gershon was quite young, and she was on a call that he wanted her to end. He tried to stop the conversation by bending the phone cord and squeezing it together, like you'd do with a garden hose to stop the flow of water. Wish I could have seen that!)

In this instance, he insisted she hang up the phone, making it clear he needed to talk to her. Upon hearing what had happened, she instantly called the police. They were able to find the man, although, in retrospect, I cannot imagine how.

I don't recall being questioned by the police, or if he was arrested, or if anything happened as a result of the encounter. If my parents pressed charges of any kind, I was not privy to that information. It was deeply unsettling, but to know that my big brother felt protective enough of me to take action and make sure I was safe was surprising and made me love him all the more. That was one of two times I recall Gershon demonstrating any care or concern for me, and I assumed it meant he loved me. That assumption carried me through the remainder of my childhood.

Gershon married quite young. He met Adrienne at a summer camp in White Plains, N.Y., where they both worked. As a fourteen-year-old, I thought she was the prettiest, sexiest girl I'd ever met. Her eyes were a captivating hazel color I'd never seen before, and she had a fabulous way of doing her eye makeup. That, combined with a husky, sultry voice, had me smitten. I always wanted a sister and she was going to be my sister-in-law! Close enough!

I distinctly remember a lime green suede jacket Adrienne wore with her jeans. I'd never seen, let alone touched suede, and it made me think that she was not only beautiful and sexy, but so chic. Sometime later, when she bought herself a new jacket, she gave me the suede one which I cherished for years.

Gershon and Adrienne got married at Leonard's of Great Neck on Long Island, where Adrienne was from. We woke up in our hotel the morning of the wedding in February 1968 to three inches of snow. By the time the wedding was over, but before the reception began, cars were covered by three feet.

Leonard's was an ostentatious event venue with multiple banquet halls but no overnight accommodations or kitchen for preparing food, just storing or heating what was brought in by caterers. There were small furnished rooms for brides and their bridal party to prepare for the wedding, or for the bar or bat mitzvah boy or girl to change into their finery before their blowout party began.

We were snowed in for three days. The bride and groom, a bar mitzvah boy, and all their respective bands, entertainers, and combined family and guests numbering in the hundreds were unable to leave Leonard's. The bands played all night, people danced into the wee hours, and I learned something about Ira, nineteen at the time, that I never knew. He was a fabulous dancer. He danced until morning with anyone who would accept his invitation, and I don't believe anyone turned him down. I was floored.

For three days, people slept on chairs placed end-to-end, on the floor, under pianos, on tables, and any flat surface they could find, using coats and tablecloths for blankets. The wedding was written up in the local New York papers.

Sitting on a couch in the living room of Gershon and Adrienne's small house, I held their newborn for the first time when he was about a month old. I felt a love I had never experienced and didn't know existed. It was astonishing and overwhelming. All in a rush of rapturous emotion, I knew if this was how I felt holding my nephew, the emotion of holding my own child would be exponentially more intense. I was overcome with anticipation of the joy I would feel in that moment, however far off it might be. Yet another epiphany cementing my desire to be a mom.

Gershon's and Adrienne's marriage, sadly, didn't last. They divorced when their youngest, Josh, was nearly two years old. I believe the abuse my brother suffered, which, in my opinion, he never came to terms with, prevented him from being a successful partner to his wife and father to his boys. I think the effects of the abuse caused him to alienate the most important people in his life. I can't claim to understand the psychological dynamics at play, or say whether I'm even close to accurate in my assessment—but over the years, everyone—from his sons, to me, to our parents, to Ira, to close friends, to women with whom he had loving relationships —was pushed away. Some friends were excised, and a few others found their way back to friendship.

My parents would not accept the alienation, and found a way to maintain relationships with him. He and Ira had not spoken for years. (Happily, at the time of this writing, they have reconnected and begun what might be a tenuous reconciliation.) Sadly, Gershon has had no contact of any kind with his sons in years. Truly heartbreaking.

As we got older, Gershon and I had a strained and, at times, extremely contentious relationship. Going for long stretches without speaking, one lasting fifteen years, we occasionally managed to reconcile, until the next blowout. We share many sensibilities, and throughout my life, I longed for a loving, close relationship. But abuse causes long-term damage when it is not or cannot be overcome. Scar tissue is hard to penetrate.

CHAPTER 7
IRA

Like my dad, I know from photographs of Ira as a child that he was beautiful. (If only I had half the good looks as the men in my family.) When Ira was in elementary school, one of his teachers called my parents to report some mischief he'd caused in class, and my mother asked what she did to discipline him. The teacher admitted that when he looked at her with his gorgeous brown eyes and smiled, she couldn't bring herself to reprimand him. It was then my parents realized he would get away with a great deal as a kid, which he did.

Once he became a young teenager, Ira found a way to escape. It seemed he was always elsewhere, spending little time at home. How he managed his absence, I'll never know. My Uncle Bill dubbed him "Mysterious Moe" because he was utterly inscrutable. No one ever knew what he was thinking, feeling, or even where he was, let alone what he might be up to. And then he'd appear as a mirage, sweetly smiling and perfectly angelic.

As kids, we were all required to play a musical instrument. I played the violin, Ira the trumpet, and Gershon the clarinet. I don't know how my parents stood it, but after dinner every week night we had to practice for an hour. We practiced simultaneously—I upstairs in my room, Ira in the kitchen, and Gershon in the unfinished basement by the boiler. At least he was warm.

Once a week, we were expected to perform in the kitchen after dinner for my parents and grandmother, who lived with us, seated at the table, along with the two of us waiting our turn to play. Often attempting the same song week after week, I scratched out "Clair de Lune," Ira blared "When the Saints Go Marching In," and Gershon's clarinet squawked, "I'm in the Mood for Love." With notes bending ever so slightly but enough to cause pain, many never reaching their destination, none were well-played.

Luckily for my dad, he was profoundly tone-deaf, but truly loved music and thought we were all prodigies. My mother and I, having good ears for music, knew better. Ira was so embarrassed to play for the family, he would either stand with his back to us or with his eyes closed and one hand on top of his head.

Ira developed a temper that would slowly smolder, which he'd sometimes struggle to tamp down, managing in most cases to keep it just below the surface. Occasionally, something would launch him into the stratosphere. One such occasion was on an evening when my parents had gone out. Gershon committed the unforgivable sin of changing the station while Ira was watching TV.

Sitting at the kitchen table after dinner, Ira was watching something on the small TV that sat on top of the portable dishwasher in the kitchen. The very TV on which we watched the horrors of the Vietnam War unfold. Whether he was simply not thinking or deliberately trying to tick him off, Gershon came and flipped the dial while Ira was in the middle of a show. That was it.

Ira chased Gershon around the house until he caught him and wrestled him to the floor. Gershon managed to turn the tables and pin Ira down with his knees on his shoulders. Our Jack Russell/Beagle, McDuff, was running in circles, jumping back and forth across Ira and Gershon, barking his head off in a scene of utter bedlam.

I saw all reason leave Ira's eyes as they glazed over with rage. My memory here is incorrect as I seem to recall him reaching back over his head, grabbing a poker, swinging it around wildly, and threatening to hit Gershon in the head. The thing is, we didn't have a fireplace.

Gershon managed to get up from the floor, grab me by the hand, and pull me out of the house onto the front porch. This was the second time my big brother behaved protectively toward his little sister, and it wasn't lost on me that he did.

Ira proceeded to lock the front and back doors, turn on every light in the house, move a chair from the dining room into the middle of the living room, and sit there for what seemed like hours, ignoring our entreaties to let us in. It was the dead of winter, and Pittsburgh tended to get chilly. He would not open the door until my parents came home. We had to hang out at the neighbor's until my folks returned. That was Ira's temper.

Meanwhile, the draft for the war was in place. Gershon was deferred due to his asthma, but Ira had a very low number in the lottery, creating the terrifying likelihood that he would be drafted. I never learned how my dad managed it, but he was able to enlist Ira in the Coast Guard Reserves. As with many things relating to my brothers, my memory is fuzzy, but I recall him spending six months or so stationed somewhere.

Gershon's recollection is that Ira came home changed, somehow, but that didn't register with me. Ira seemed customarily quiet, often sullen, and deeply detached. Nothing new. He left Pittsburgh soon after ending his stint with the Reserves to move to western Massachusetts with a friend. He ended up making his life there, where he got married, divorced, and married again. Ira's second wife, Mary, had a two-year-old daughter, Beth, and they soon had a son, Alex.

Similar to my relationship with Gershon, I cannot recall much engagement with Ira as we were growing up. He and I have had our struggles, though none as protracted as those Gershon and I have been through. There was a particularly rough patch when our mom died, and while we have come back to one another, the fallout from that time is that our families are not nearly as close as I would like. But we do the best we can, which sometimes is the best we can hope for.

Writing this book has been a revelatory experience. Therapeutic. Enlightening. Cathartic. I've come to a deeper understanding and resolution of several of my life's greater mysteries. Light has been shed on my many missteps and misguided choices. Amongst the most revealing has been my insight into how unfulfilling relationships with the males in my family left me feeling, to varying degrees, unloved, invisible, and inconsequential.

If my brothers loved me, I was seldom made to feel it. My dad's love was intermittently discernable, but with an inconsistent and infrequent expression, leaving me too often feeling its absence rather than its warmth. It's clear that my choices of husbands were attempts to work through unresolved issues with my dad and brothers, all in the hopes of one day grabbing the brass ring of unconditional love, acceptance, and approval.

CHAPTER 8
THE PATERNAL PARADOX

I believe it started around fourth grade. A recurring nightmare lasting years. I became as nocturnal as possible, dreading sleep, knowing it would appear soon after I closed my eyes. In spite of my great effort to stay awake, I'd fall asleep, of course, and there it was. It began in color, walking with my dad up a beautiful grassy hill behind my elementary school on a sun-soaked day with an impossibly azure sky.

I'm about six years old, blissfully holding my daddy's hand, going for a lovely walk, just the two of us. We'd reach the crest of the hill and stop. Here, the dream faded from vivid, saturated, glorious color to stark, bleak, black and white.

We stand there, staring at the abyss at our feet. Like a visibly and rapidly metastasizing cancer, it spreads out in all directions, slithering ever-outward and down into eternity. Scrap metal forms an impenetrable thicket below us of twisted railroad tracks, deformed roller-coaster rails, buckled girders, and all manner of rusted, warped, misshapen metal.

My dad lets go of my hand and fearlessly jumps down, landing on the tracks. Happily scampering from track to rail to girder and back again while magically maintaining his balance, he encourages me to follow. I'm paralyzed. The terror in my throat is choking me. The longer I hesitate, the angrier he gets and the more labored my breathing becomes.

He's screaming at me now, shouting that if I don't follow him, I'll be in big trouble. I cannot speak or move, fully cognizant that I'm doomed if I do, and doomed if I don't. If I don't follow him, I destroy all hope of ever winning his love. If I do, I plummet to my death.

The dream ends with no resolution. I remain immobilized at the edge of the abyss while my dad continues hopping about, growing increasingly angry as he admonishes me to obey. I wonder if, at some point, his wrath will crescendo, if the moment will arrive at which he can feel no greater fury. That moment does not come. His rage knows no bounds. I suppose it's fair to conclude that choosing survival, despite my deep-seated desire for his approval, revealed my instinct for self-preservation and belief that I would endure, even at the risk of losing his love.

And then there were the sublime moments when my father became the loving dad I knew he was deep down. Sprinkled throughout my childhood, these moments were instrumental in empowering me to come out of it all, loving him with my whole heart, able to forgive his failures.

From the time I was seven, I began begging my parents for a pony. It doesn't get more clichéd than that, but I desperately wanted one. Needless to say, our tiny row house with no property did not lend itself to pony ownership. My parents asked where we would keep the pony and where I would ride it. I assumed these questions indicated consideration of my pleadings. With great optimism and enthusiasm, I said we could put hay on the floor and keep him in the basement, and I'd ride him to school and the market and the drugstore up the street.

I finally had to accept the hard truth. There would be no pony on Wightman Street. Instead, my dad informed me he would take me once a week for riding lessons. I was dumbfounded. And deliriously excited.

Every Saturday morning, he drove me to stables two hours away. For eight weeks, he sacrificed his Saturdays for me. It meant more to me than anything in the world. He sat in the indoor corral, with the sun streaming in through windows high in the walls, causing everything in its path to sparkle with glittering joy. He watched as I rode for an hour, then piled me back in the car for the long ride home. Notably and inexplicably, he allowed my muddy boots into his most prized and pristine possession, his baby blue Buick LeSabre, where we chatted about the lesson and talked about Sparky, my horse, behaving like any fully functional loving father and daughter. And everything else dissipated, like stale air that would never return. It was magnificent to see my dad as I believed he truly was, and from time to precious time, bask in the warmth of his love.

Those Saturdays made me want children all the more. As I got older, that special time caused me to pine for motherhood with a partner capable of expressing nothing but love for his children, so my kids could have only splendid experiences with their dad.

CHAPTER 9
SARAH HEARTBURN ENTERS MY BODY

Much of the power I inherited from my mom manifested itself as a performer. As my nascent Drama Princess emerged, my mother dubbed me Sarah Heartburn, after the famous silent film star Sarah Bernhardt, known for melodrama and histrionics. At every opportunity, I expressed myself in over-the-top theatrics, earning the moniker. My tiny size made it all the more ridiculous and, I guess, hilarious. I was a big entertainer in a little body.

By the age of six or seven, I was regaling everyone at family gatherings, obligated to listen and fawn, belting out such favorites as "I Enjoy Being a Girl" from *Flower Drum Song* and "Honey Bun" from *South Pacific*. At home, I'd stand on an overturned metal wastebasket in the upstairs bathroom so I could gaze into the mirror while singing "Younger than Springtime" because it made me cry. I loved to watch myself emote.

A long-sleeved turtleneck with the collar around my head and the body and sleeves hanging down my back simulated waist-length flowing tresses, since the cloud of kink on my crown poorly impersonating hair was a constant humiliation. I would dance around my room, causing my "hair" to sway to and fro, singing at the top of my little lungs something from some musical or other. I was the bomb.

And speaking of bombs, in the fifth grade my friend and I blew up her basement. Unfortunately, and much to our surprise, we were in it at the time. An assignment from our science teacher gone horribly awry had us "experimenting" in Debbie's brother's amateur science lab in their cellar. His strict instructions never to go in without him went unheeded.

The walls in the cinder block room were lined with metal shelving where beakers, test tubes, and glass containers of all shapes and sizes were neatly placed, some full of unknown liquids, powders, and who knew what all. We were giddy, as we knew we shouldn't be in there at all, let alone doing what we were doing. She and I both loved adventures, especially the kind that involved misbehaving, and this was that in spades.

Grabbing a few small bottles from the shelves, we mixed a bit of this liquid and a dash of that powder in a small ceramic dish on a counter, waiting to see what chemical reactions might result. Adding a drop of some sort of fluid from a different bottle made the mixture begin to bubble, then smoke slightly, and change color as we watched, transfixed, and insanely excited.

Then, in a massive stroke of stupidity, we decided it was a great idea to apply heat in the form of lit matches to the gurgling solution. Apparently, our combined IQs fell just below that of Beavis and Butthead. In a horrific, flashing moment came the loudest boom I'd ever heard. It sent me running in terror out of the lab, where I stood with my face pressed up against a wall, my hands over my ears, for what felt like a short eternity.

When I was able to open my eyes and the smoke had cleared, I could see that every single glass container on the shelves had shattered. And Debbie was nowhere in sight. As the ringing in my ears diminished and my hearing slowly returned, I heard blood-curdling screams. Realizing she was upstairs, I ran as fast as I could up the steps. There stood Debbie in the kitchen with a bloodied face and blackened hands, frantically grabbing at her hair that was thickly matted with blood. Her mom had been upstairs and came running when she heard the blast. Panic-stricken, she was in another world from which she could not help her daughter.

Finally, a small sliver of Ruth's ability to reason returned, enabling her to call a neighbor who came and took Debbie to the hospital. Ruth was unaware of my presence. She was submerged in her own tortured universe. I left the house and made the thirty-minute trek to the store my mom worked in. I distinctly remember hanging onto my sanity by my fingernails as I talked out loud to myself the entire time I walked, repeating, "Don't let her die. Don't let her die."

Terrified of triggering my dad, I was afraid to go home, which was much closer than my mother's store. It was my mom I needed. When she saw me come in, she ushered me to the back, where, in hysterics, I told her what had happened. She loaded me in the car and took me to the hospital.

I had been standing behind Debbie at the time of the explosion, so my injuries were minimal. She spent three weeks in the hospital. Glass had blown into her eye, necessitating surgery. It lacerated the left side of her face, and all the way down the left side of her body. Once Debbie was allowed visitors, our friends and I would sneak into the hospital having applied full faces of makeup, teased our hair way up high, and stuffed our bras with socks so we looked sixteen, the minimum age for visitors. Well... we thought we looked sixteen. In retrospect, we looked like eleven-year-old prostitutes.

Our teacher was summarily fired, but Debbie and I became fairly famous. Rather than realizing what a close call I'd encountered and how lethal a bullet I'd dodged, I think the experience filled me with a perverse sense of invincibility, when it should've taught me how fragile life is and how vulnerable we all are. The intersection of fragile and vulnerable was not a place I liked to spend time.

As undeterred by trauma as ever, I did what I always did. I stuffed it all down as deep as I could and muscled my way through, carrying on with my little complicated life. I resumed performing at every opportunity throughout the remainder of middle, junior, and high school, starring in *Funny Girl*, *Bye Bye, Birdie*, *I Do! I Do!*, *The Boyfriend*, *Mame*, and various one-act plays. Auditions were held for each production, and as Sarah Heartburn and a version of Barbra Streisand were cohabiting in me, I usually landed the lead.

One production I starred in had been accepted into a drama festival held annually at the YM&WHA, the Jewish equivalent of the YMCA. The Jewish Community Center in Squirrel Hill, the hub of our social life, offered clubs, sororities, and fraternities, and each was invited to enter a one-act play in the festival.

The Y was a beautiful early twentieth-century stone building with a huge auditorium housing an enormous stage. Our club, the Jades, entered a seriously esoteric play in the festival, entitled *The Shewing-Up of Blanco Posnet*, by George Bernard Shaw, first produced in 1909. It doesn't get more esoteric than that.

I was in ninth grade, playing Feemy Evans, the town harlot. My mother made my costume, as she did for every production—this one made of fabric from an old nightgown of hers that she had dyed red for the occasion, complete with a deep-cut V-neck. Ron Nash, the director, in the midst of getting his master's in theater from Carnegie Mellon, imagined that Feemy sported quite the chest. Jodi Mitchel, however, did not. So Ron had me draw cleavage on myself, which basically made me look like I had bad bruises between my boobs, such as they were.

I must have delivered a riveting performance, as I won the Best Actress award at the festival that year. Now, there could be no question... I was destined for greatness. (This is as good a time as any to tell you that at my recent fifty-third high school reunion—our fiftieth was derailed by COVID—a classmate actually told me I was his greatest disappointment. In an uncharacteristic show of restraint, I did not assault him. He went on to explain that he always assumed I'd become a Broadway star. My star didn't travel much beyond Squirrel Hill.)

I never had so much fun in my life as I did performing, and was never happier. Rather than being relegated to invisibility and inconsequence, as I so often was at home, at least in the eyes of my dad and brothers, I was in the spotlight. Literally. All eyes were on me. I reveled in it. And as I was fairly talented, thanks to my mom, the attention was all positive. It wasn't like I got noticed for being pregnant or a convicted shoplifter or doing who knows what with boys under the stairwell. I was winning awards and accolades. Even my brothers sat up and took notice, and my dad expressed pride in me. It was pure heaven and, as it later turned out, the pinnacle of my career.

To be seen, heard, and—dare I say—admired likely saved me from a life of self-imposed oblivion. A fascinating parallel is that, in a sense, my dad and I lived double lives. His true nature was abundantly apparent with colleagues and friends. He was kind, loving, giving, sentimental, and sweet. Had we let on that he was a tyrant in the house, no one would've believed us. Roy Mitchel raise his voice, let alone a hand? I don't think so.

And I was a different person on the outside. Not to say my fury didn't make appearances in school. I was a big-mouthed troublemaker, rebellious and loud, all in a desperate attempt to make my presence felt. But I was also funny and, as a performer, able to offer mitigating qualities to friends and even teachers, so as not to be seen as just another pain in the ass, which I was in maddening measure.

I was constantly kicked out of the classroom, made to sit in the hall due to misbehavior, or sent down to the principal's office. During a half-day assembly in middle school, my besties and I sat in the auditorium when a teacher came and called me out, saying I was wanted in the office. I had no idea what I'd done this time.

When I saw the principal, Hedwig O. Pregler (no kidding), she told me I would be tested for the Workshop, the accelerated program for advanced students. After two hours, she sent me back to the assembly. Still disbelieving, and more than a little proud, I scribbled a note and passed it to my friends. I could barely sit still as they each read it and handed it to the next. It said, *"Oh my God! Oh my God! Oh my God! I was just tested for the Workshop. From now on, I'm going to be a perfect little angle!"* Perhaps, had I known how to spell "angel," I would've been deemed Workshop-worthy. As it was, not so much.

It was late one afternoon and Ava, my best friend since second grade, was at the house when my mom called to say her car died and she would be late getting home. She asked me to start dinner.

Ava was sitting at the little kitchen table with a yellow patterned top and chrome legs, on a yellow vinyl chair with matching legs, set into the tiny alcove. I was at the stove when I wondered aloud, unfortunately, "What the *fuck* is wrong with that car?"

As "fuck" hung in the air, my father appeared in the kitchen, just getting home from work. Inflated nearly to bursting upon hearing his daughter say the word of all forbidden words, he seemed to have swelled to thirty times his normal size, much like the Stay-Puft Marshmallow Man in *Ghostbusters*, but with a different facial expression. Ava thought it was the funniest thing she'd ever seen and was laughing her head off. I, however, found the situation less than humorous. I knew what was coming.

When my dad's admonishment reached a deafening level, Ava wisely left the house. Blinded by his rage, my dad lunged at me, and I had the good sense and reflexes to run.

The farthest I could get was upstairs to my bedroom, which I shared with my grandmother. Seconds later, he exploded into the room with his belt already off. Terrified, I put my grandmother's double bed between us but had pretty much trapped myself between the bed and the wall. With his remaining shred of sanity, he slammed the bed repeatedly with his belt instead of me.

"Where'd you hear a word like that?" he screamed. "Not in this house! Whores use words like that. Are you a whore?" Strangely, what struck me was his pronunciation of "whore." It sounded like "whoore," a pronunciation I'd never heard. I found it interesting that he would say it that way.

By focusing on that ridiculous detail, I was able to distract myself from the unfolding horror. He finally left the room, banging the door so hard the windows rattled. It took some time for him to cool off. And it took some time for me to stuff the resentment and outrage into my internal denial drawer. Of course, the incident was never spoken of.

Finally, and miraculously, I managed to graduate high school with a peace sign emblazoned on my mortar board, good hippy that I was. Not unhappy to be leaving home, I went off to Ohio University, which proved to be a total waste of the debt my folks took on to send me. That was guilt I never resolved.

Little studying. *Lots* of drugs. Speed. LSD. Mescaline. Pot. Psilocybin. Quaaludes. And just one ton of fun... until something resembling a nervous breakdown in the last semester of my junior year stealthily crept up on me, sending me home. It felt like my identity was slipping away, and feeling the need to be in a primal place, I wanted to be where if I walked down the street, someone might say "Hi Jodi," and remind me who I was. I tried to complete my senior year at the University of Pittsburgh, but a fairly severe depression had set in, and I was unable to graduate. Hell, I was unable to get out of bed.

Living back at home—subjected to my mother's constant worry over how much I was sleeping and my dad's contempt at my lethargy—put me in a delicate emotional state. My mom decided to deploy tough love with as swift a figurative kick in the ass as she could manage. It reignited my fury and summoned Fightin' Little Jodi, who appeared, guns a' blazin', like a foul-mouthed Yosemite Sam, shootin' and shoutin', "Fuck this shit! I'm outta here!!"

I only had half my wits about me, but decided that pursuing a career as an actor was something I wanted to do. I shared that bit of news with Ron, the director from Carnegie Mellon, with whom I'd stayed in close touch after high school. He offered to help arrange an audition in the drama school at Juilliard in New York. That seemed a far cry from my capabilities, but if Ron was confident enough in me to set up an audition, who was I to argue?

At Julliard some weeks later, I was ushered into a small theater-in-the-round, with seating set in several rows around the perimeter above the stage, lending the space the look of a coliseum where the Christians met the lion. At least fifteen faculty members were seated around the theater, including John Houseman, the famously cantankerous actor who was on Juilliard's board. Under theatrical lighting, I was a total wreck as I started the first of two monologues I had prepared—one from a comedy, and another from a drama, both of my choosing.

I was so nervous that I flubbed the beginning of the first monologue and had to start again. Finally, I settled into myself and managed to complete both pieces, having absolutely no idea how well or poorly I did. Houseman thanked me on behalf of those in the audience and informed me that a decision would come down several months later. I thanked them all for their time and the opportunity, cracked some lame joke, and left the theater.

True to form, incapable of waiting for anything, I tracked Houseman down a few weeks following my audition, calling to ask if he could share any information. In a turn of great generosity and kindness, he said he and the panel agreed that Juilliard was not where I needed to be, as they felt I was ready to audition and perform. He suggested I get in front of as many producers and directors as I could. Of course, this was his diplomatic way of saying I was not Juilliard material and wishing me luck.

CHAPTER 10

THE EMERGING PERFORMER

I landed my first professional gig in Pittsburgh. If you were a fan of *Mr. Rogers' Neighborhood*, you may recall the character Chef Brockett. Don Brockett was a beloved fixture in Pittsburgh's entertainment industry. I auditioned for a cabaret show he was producing called *Amen, Amen, Etc.* to tour dinner theaters around the country. It was a musical revue featuring songs from religious-themed musicals such as *Godspell*, *Pippin*, and *Jesus Christ Superstar*. I traveled with the show for a few months, garnering good reviews, further solidifying my desire to pursue a career as a performer.

Booked at a dinner theater in Valparaiso, Indiana that summer, the cast was housed in a dorm on the Valparaiso University campus. I was awakened one morning from a deep sleep to the sound of heavy footsteps running down the hall that stopped at my door, upon which someone was pounding with all their might.

I opened the door to see a young woman standing breathless. She said, "My name is Vanessa. My room's down the hall. Someone just told me there's a Jew in here. I've never seen a Jew. Are you the Jew?"

I said, "Why, yes! I am!"

I know it'll be hard to believe, but this young woman asked me as she craned her neck to see the top of my head, "Where are your horns?" Was she that ignorant or just evil? It was literally the rudest awakening. I told her every summer, we molt and lose our horns, but they grow back in the fall. I added that I was sorry she missed them. They're quite beautiful—goldish and slightly fuzzy. Sometimes, you just have to disappoint people, especially the contemptible ones.

My next professional gig was on a Norwegian Caribbean cruise ship performing the revue with three other performers from the original show. Sailing from Charleston, South Carolina, to Bermuda and Nassau was an adventure. I was not yet twenty, and working amongst people from all over the world.

I had never been on a boat or ship of any kind and was concerned about motion sickness since, as a kid, I was prone to nausea in the car, on the dreaded Tilt a' Whirl, etc. I was doing fine until, in the midst of our first performance on the open ocean, our four standing microphones started to slowly slide to one side and then the other.

What started as a slight rocking motion of the ship became something else as we ran into thirty-foot swells. Passengers made haste to their staterooms, myself included. We were literally bouncing off the walls. I knew these conditions did not bode well for me.

I finally got into my stateroom, went into the head, and proceeded to throw up for what seemed like hours, food I swore I'd eaten a month earlier. On my knees, I held the toilet seat in place so it wouldn't bang me in the head with the rocking of the ship. And then... all my muscles contracted. And I mean con-*tract*-ed. My arms drew up to my chest, so now the toilet seat *is* banging me in the head. My hands balled into fists with my thumbs between my index and second fingers. After an eternity, certain I'd lost fifteen pounds (there's an upside to everything), the vomiting stopped.

It seemed something well beyond sea sickness was happening. I needed to call the ship's doctor. Then I discovered my legs wouldn't straighten. Unable to stand up, I crawled to the phone, miraculously managing to pull myself into a standing position. It took every ounce of strength I had to straighten my arm, open my hand, and pick up the receiver.

When someone answered and I started to speak, I realized my tongue was involved. I was now in a comedy sketch. I sounded like some bad joke about a person with a pronounced speech impediment. Finally, she understood I needed to see the doctor immediately and said, "You and everyone else onboard."

I fell back to the floor and crawled into my bunk. The doctor arrived and administered a suppository (that was fun) which instantaneously put an end to the nausea. I asked him what was wrong with me and he surmised that losing so much body fluid so quickly caused the reaction. I don't know how many years it was before I stepped foot on another boat, but I'm sure you'll understand when I say it was a while.

It was smooth sailing from that point on. As I got to know the staff, I learned that many spent nine months of the year onboard and three at home with spouses and families. It was not at all unusual for relationships to begin and, in many cases, last as long as a marriage might. There were, of course, trysts and fleeting romances, as well.

I became involved with a pianist from Hungary. I didn't ask and never knew if he was married or in a serious relationship at home. I didn't want to know. I was nineteen and, though not a virgin, as sexually inexperienced, naïve, and unworldly as a nineteen-year-old could be. What put me at a further disadvantage was coming to this relationship as I did to all encounters with men, needing, above all else, to feel loved and worthy.

Growing up as I did, I was not filled with self-respect and confidence. I possessed no strong center or sense of personal power. Quite the opposite. My emotional and psychological core was constructed on ever-shifting sands of insecurity, self-doubt, and a deep-seated belief that I didn't deserve much. From such unstable footing, it was not possible to assert myself, especially when it was most important to do so.

Villi was considerably older, and as a European man, held certain expectations and attitudes about women. Perhaps that was merely a function of who he was as a man and not necessarily a European man. I was uncomfortable during our sexual encounters, never feeling in control. I lacked any ability to say no or put a stop to anything, and I recall wanting to put the brakes on several times.

The first time our intimacy went beyond its initial level, I felt unprepared and not at all sure I wanted what was happening to happen. But as I did not have the capacity to make my discomfort known, and since Villi was not tuned into me on any level other than sexually, he either believed I was a willing participant, or gave no consideration to the question. A few weeks before my twentieth birthday, I went home to discover I was pregnant. And most importantly, I learned what a remarkable man my father was.

Somehow, I was able to tell my parents. I'm really not sure where I found the courage to do that, but it was borne of necessity. In the most striking paradox, my dad's Jekyll-and-Hyde nature was revealed in all its complexity. The person who struck the greatest anger, frustration, yearning, trepidation, fear, and apprehension in me my whole life was the person who came to my rescue in my most vulnerable moment as a young woman and assured me he would find a way to obtain an abortion.

Pre-*Roe v. Wade*, he learned that the procedure was not legal in Pennsylvania, but was in New York. Having located a clinic in Niagara Falls, he and my mom drove me to upstate New York, stayed with me in the clinic, and got me through the ordeal. To this day, I do not know how he found the information and never knew how to repay them for their stunning display of support and unconditional love.

Not realizing the physical and emotional toll of what I'd just been through, we decided to see the Falls after the procedure. You know, so it shouldn't be a total loss. Of course, after spending an entire day sightseeing following an abortion, I ended up in quite a bit of pain, bleeding more than I otherwise would have. A call to the clinic put our minds at ease that this was normal, but I needed to stay off my feet longer than we planned. Fortunately, we were able to return home several days later.

There was never again a question in my heart that my father loved me deeply, despite his struggles and deficiencies as a dad. This experience, beyond all others, enabled me to forgive him for everything, if not rid myself of their effects.

I took the time I needed to regroup and recover, finally feeling ready to contemplate my next move. I was working and dating again, seeing a guy with a good friend in L.A. who was a screenwriter. Buddy said he would be happy to introduce me to David when he was in town. When we met, David offered to connect me with some people in the industry in L.A. should I decide to come out, but he couldn't promise what might come of any of those connections. Sounded reasonable. He offered me a place to stay until I could find an apartment.

CHAPTER 11
WHAT HAPPENS IN L.A....

I wanted my parents to meet David and hear about his plan to help me. The four of us sat in the living room one evening when he came to meet my folks and tell them how he thought he could support my efforts in Los Angeles. I could crash with him until I found my own place, and he would introduce me to professionals in the business. It was a lovely evening and an interesting conversation. My mom and dad thanked him for coming and his willingness to help me.

Then, in a what-the-fuck-were-they-thinking moment, said it all sounded like a good plan to them. Had I been listening hard enough, I probably would have heard David salivating. I was twenty. He was forty. And single. Did a red flag appear in anybody's peripheral vision anywhere along the way, including mine? Nope. I packed my naïveté and headed out to L.A.

On the plane, it occurred to me that David might think I would be sleeping with him. Duh. Well, I had to put the kibosh on that, so before we left the L.A. airport, I suggested we get a cup of coffee. I told him I would not be going to bed with him and if that posed a problem, I could stay with a friend of my parents. He said, "Of course, no worries. I'll sleep on the couch.

"OK," I said. "Let's go!"

Later that night, I sat on my suitcase in David's driveway, waiting to be rescued by my parents' friend. To my folks' great credit, as I cried on the phone to them every night for three weeks, they encouraged me to ride it out, confident I would settle in. Settle in I did, finally able to venture out and rent my first apartment.

My flare for interior design was on full display. If I had a business, it would've been called "Why Bother Interiors." Paula Ruth gently queried upon visiting for the first time, "Sweetheart, when will you accept the fact that you live here?" Next to no furniture, except a bed. But I was dead serious about my beds.

Growing up in Squirrel Hill, six of us lived in a tiny three-bedroom row house where, as you know, I shared a room with my grandmother. The bedrooms were the size of Chiclets. Nana slept in a double bed, which left just enough room for a roll-away cot for me. So comfortable. Of course, in college, there were only twin beds, so finally having my own place, I was determined to get the biggest bed I could find.

My penchant for sleep developed early on. That recurring nightmare turned me into an avowed night owl, but once I got to sleep, I loved sleeping almost more than anything in life. Still do. I'd set my alarm on Saturday mornings so I wouldn't miss cartoons, and every single Saturday when the alarm clock blared, I'd knock it off the nightstand, roll over, and blissfully fall back to sleep. My ardency for sleep was deeply ingrained as a kid by my Nana's morning routine.

On weekends, I'd lie in the roll-away, fitfully trying to sleep in, while Nana grunted and groaned as she struggled to stuff her abundant belly and voluminous breasts into a size zero girdle and bra large enough to transport twin missiles. Then she'd sit down and pant for a while.

The next order of business after putting on her stockings, clothes, and shoes, was styling what little there was of her hair with a tiny plastic thing she bought from the door-to-door Fuller Brush salesman. After brushing for an eternity came the Aqua Net hair spray. She circled her head twenty-eight times and not one rotation less; the can hissing louder than a seventeen-foot anaconda. She then used a small comb to clear out the six strands stuck in the brush, which was probably accomplished in the first two swipes, but she continued for fifty-seven. So fast and so loud. *Pppphh-hhttt! Pppphhhhttt! Pppphhhhttt!* Over and over and over and over.

If I wasn't awakened by her grunting or panting or *pppphhhhttting*, I woke up choking on Aqua Net. And if that didn't do it, the thousands of tiny kisses she'd deposit on my cheek before leaving the room did. As my furious eyes fluttered open, she'd say with great surprise, "Oh, honey! Did I wake you?"

Now in my own apartment, foreshadowing my nearly furniture-less Manhattan apartment a few years later, sharing no space with anyone and with nothing but glorious potential spread out in all directions, my next big goal was to obtain the largest bed possible. That, however, was a challenge, since I had no disposable income. How lucky was it when I learned that Goodwill sold refurbished double beds for twenty-five dollars, advertised as rebuilt and sanitized. My ticket to luxury! I jumped at the chance and decided to make the first big purchase for my new, all-to-myself apartment.

I called Goodwill and ordered my mattress, ecstatic that I would soon be sleeping in my first gigantic double bed. All that remained was awaiting delivery of my nocturnal oasis. At noon on a Saturday came a knock at the door.

Tumbling out of bed, I pushed my trusty knee-sock-turned-sleep-mask up on my forehead, causing my matted hair to stand up a good distance from my scalp, with the eye makeup from the night before I had not been inclined to remove when I got home at 3 a.m. halfway down my cheeks. A vision, I answered the door.

There stood an enormous man filling the doorway. Surely an apparition, my Giant Goodwill Sleep Fairy was about to bestow upon me unsurpassed nighttime bliss. He said in a deeper-than-deep, uncanny Barry White impersonation, "I've got your mattress."

I invited him in with unbridled anticipation and gleefully watched as he took my old mattress into the hall and set up my "new" bed. I paid and thanked him profusely. He left without a word.

In the course of two weeks, the stuffing in my "new" mattress silently shifted. I was soon sleeping in the wedge of a V-shaped mattress-turned-trough. Cranky, I called Goodwill to complain about the shifting innards of my mattress, and they agreed to send a "new" used one at no cost. The following Saturday, at noon, came a knock on the door. There stood my silent Sleep Fairy.

With my knee-sock around my head, the small mountain of hair rising from my scalp, doing my spot-on Alice Cooper, he looked at me and deadpanned, "You lookin' lovely, as usual." I like to make an impression.

When I told the story to a friend, she said her favorite part was my expectation of customer service from Goodwill like you'd find at Bergdorf. Hey, you don't ask, you don't get.

Soon after settling into L.A., Passover arrived. A few hours before the first Seder would begin, it became clear how important my Jewish identity was to me. Knowing my entire family would be gathering at our house later that afternoon, the thought of not observing the holiday with them all was more than a little upsetting. I figured if I had my own little Seder, I would feel slightly less lonesome and disconnected from my family.

I flew into action, dug out my phonebook (for those of you who know what that is), found a listing for a Jewish shop, and called. I described my sad situation and asked if they carried Haggadahs—the book containing the Seder service—holiday candles, and most importantly, Manischewitz Concord Grape wine, which many the world over consider to be the greatest failure in the history of winemaking.

To my delight, I was told they had everything I needed and would keep the store open if I could get there within the hour. I rushed to the shop where the elderly, incredibly sweet owner seemed proud of me for wanting to observe the holiday.

During the course of a Seder, participants recite a prayer over wine and drink four cups, as they're called. I'm not much of a wine drinker, but I can drink Manischewitz 'til the kosher cows come home. And I saw nothing wrong with having four rather large cups since my Uncle Bill wasn't there to stop me.

Sitting at the card table in the sparsely equipped kitchen, I conducted my own little solo Seder, complete with a thrown-together Seder plate containing the best stand-ins I could come up with for the ritual foods: a bowl of chicken-flavored water aspiring to be chicken soup (alas, none of Nana's matzah balls); the requisite gefilte fish, that no self-respecting—or sane—gentile would even consider sampling, replete with horseradish; room-temperature, tough chicken; and matzah slathered in butter, which is the only way to protect yourself from choking as you struggle to swallow —since every last drop of saliva has been sucked into the matzah, which is still nowhere near moist.

Jewish observances begin at sundown so given the time difference, my family's Seder had ended well before mine had. I called home and my mom, thrilled to hear from me, was happy to chat. I told her all about my lovely, lonesome little Seder. It was beyond wonderful to hear my mom's voice during my favorite Jewish holiday. Eight words in, she realized I was drunk. *I* didn't realize I was drunk. As lovely as my little solo Seder was, this warm, loving conversation cemented my resolve never to miss another Passover in Pittsburgh.

Having headed for points as distant as possible without leaving the country, L.A. provided the setting at a time when I needed to turn off my mind and live on my own terms, with abandon—even, perhaps especially, if it meant living dangerously. And I was very good at it. Finally landing a job that lasted for a while, I was soon waiting tables at the well-known Improv in Hollywood. Serving by night and pursuing a career in the entertainment industry by day meant a hectic schedule. There were lots of drugs to ingest and much sex to have. It was, after all, the '80s.

I was a singing server, taking off my apron, putting down my tray, and performing in between comedy sets from soon-to-become legends like Robin Williams, Jay Leno, and Andy Kaufman, then waiting on superstars such as Johnny Carson and Richard Pryor.

The Improv's main room was quite dark, with long rows of tables arranged perpendicular to the semi-circular stage in a sort of half hub and spokes setup. There was always a very long line of people waiting to be let in, who then entered and were seated all at once. As a server, it was quite challenging, as your station, no matter how large, was instantly full of hungry people, eager to start drinking and be entertained. It was such a cool atmosphere. The audience was so close to the performers, and they got to see some of the very best in the business.

Robin Williams had just begun in the role of Mork on the hugely popular TV show *Mork and Mindy* and was an absolute force of nature. He was also the sweetest guy I'd ever met. He worked out material with a process mostly consisting of freeform riffing and in-the-moment stream-of-consciousness ad-libbing. It was clearly evident we were in the presence of genius, and everyone knew it. To have witnessed his unparalleled talent and rocketing career trajectory was something I'll never forget.

Also unforgettable was an evening at the posh Beverly Wilshire Hotel, where I attended a gala banquet dinner with my folks who were in town for a conference and convention in my dad's industry. They invited me to join them. The huge, ornate lobby was packed. Standing with my parents, all dolled up in a sleek silver and black polka-dotted floor-length dress, I caught sight of Robin across the lobby, and he eyed me. By now, everyone knew who Robin Williams was and were whispering to and poking one another, bringing more and more attention to his presence.

In a signature Robin move with a flair for high drama, he loudly gasped when he saw me, rose up on his toes, leaned back, arms in the air, and rushed across the very large lobby to my side. He threw his arms around me and, leaning me way over backward, kissed me in a long, exaggerated, theatrical display. He then stood me up as everyone in the room asked one another, "Who is she??" Of course, no one knew who I was because I was nobody, but for a moment, many thought I must be someone. Shit! *I* thought I must be someone! He then disappeared as fast as he'd appeared, and my parents and I went into the ballroom for dinner.

Richard Pryor was the other genius in the club whose career was at the time much more established than Robin's. Being in proximity to Richard Pryor was like being in the presence of royalty, which is exactly what he was in the entertainment world. Everyone spoke in softer tones, and occasionally someone approached his table to pay their respects and gush.

He graciously spoke with everyone, all of whom left his table starry-eyed and transfixed. I served him a five-dollar drink for which he tipped me twenty dollars. The Improv, and the world, reeled at the tragic and desperately premature departure of this supremely gifted, tortured soul.

Andy Kaufman was simply the strangest human I'd ever met. His comedy was like no other and he often lived in character offstage, leaving folks to wonder who was the real Andy Kaufman. I loved seeing people struggle to know what to make of him and his comedy. It was intriguing to watch him develop the character of Latka Gravas on *Taxi* which made him famous. He was a fully committed performance artist, living his art at all times. There was little separation between Andy and his myriad characters. He was fascinating. And he, too, passed away much before his time.

Jay Leno, with his star rapidly rising, was the nicest, most unassuming guy, and I adored him. He used to love to walk past me at the Improv and make hilarious, off-the-cuff, and what would now be considered wildly inappropriate comments, such as "We've got to get you out of these wet things. You'll catch your death!" Or "That's such a pretty sweater. It would look great hanging over the chair in my bedroom." One night after work, he rode me up Mulholland Drive on the back of his motorcycle to a spot with a breathtaking view of L.A. sparkling below and said, "Stick with me, kid, and you'll be farting through silk."

There was a small glass-enclosed section in the back of the main room of the Improv where the biggest muckety-mucks would be seated, like Carson. He was just too famous to engage with anyone. He came in with his entourage, sat in the "booth," watched performers to see who might be ripe for *The Tonight Show*, and left. It was always incredibly exciting to see people I knew appear on the show and watch their careers launch into the stratosphere.

Sometime later, during my back-and-forth phase, I had moved to Manhattan and was waiting tables at the New York Improv, where I met and started dating Larry David. He did very occasional stand-up before Seinfeld was on the air, and was simply the funniest person I ever saw. Consumed by triviality, Larry was a keen, misanthropic observer of life in its most banal absurdity, primarily obsessed with those aspects of humanity as minuscule and inconsequential as they could possibly be. That's exactly what makes him ridiculously funny—humor about nothing.

We'd been dating for six months when he broke it off. It seemed to me that things were going swimmingly. We spent the lion's share of our time together in hysterics. He explained, however, that he needed to end it. "Why?" I asked.

His answer: "You remind me of my mother."

Mind you, I was twenty-three and nowhere near resembling a Jewish mother—not that I could tell, at least. But Larry David's mind works in mysterious ways. As did his neighbor's.

Larry lived in a New York City apartment complex in the theater district called the Manhattan Plaza, built to provide subsidized housing to people in the entertainment industry. Kenny Kramer, of *Seinfeld* fame, upon whom the character Kramer was based, lived across the hall. Well after Larry and I split up, I went out with Kramer a few times. That was short-lived. He was just a tad too insane.

Some months later, I needed to move out of my apartment but wanted to remain in New York to continue to pursue work. Kramer agreed to sublet his apartment to me, as he was planning to be out of town for an extended period.

His apartment was memorable and later immortalized. Every surface —walls, floors, ceilings—had been carpeted in a light maroon shag.

Kramer had decided to get rid of all of his furniture and built a boxed-in bench around the perimeter of his living room, also carpeted. Throw pillows adorned the bench. Any of this ring a bell to you *Seinfeld* fans?

Kramer's bed, consisting of only a mattress, lay atop a boxed-in platform built on one wall of his bedroom, four feet off the floor, also carpeted on three sides. Two carpeted steps led up to the top of the platform. At the foot of his mattress facing it stood a full-size suit of armor, complete with helmet, gauntlets, and sabatons, a spear in one hand and poleax in the other.

Waking up at 3 a.m. my first night in the apartment, as my eyes slowly opened in the dimly lit room, I heard someone screaming. It was me. I had forgotten about the knight at the foot of the bed. Looming over me, it looked like an 8-foot-tall alien standing motionless, watching me sleep. Luckily, I was able to stop screaming before anyone heard me.

Larry and I remained good and close friends and hung out together regularly. Once *Seinfeld* was well on its way, we drove his mom home from Manhattan to Long Island. She was a tiny woman who didn't smile the entire time we spent together. I began to catch glimpses of Larry David's origins.

At one point along the way, I turned toward the backseat and said, "Mrs. David, you must be incredibly proud of Larry and his success with *Seinfeld*!"

She said, "It's fascinating. I never thought he was that funny." In the space of two short sentences, she completed the picture of how Larry became Larry. He found his mother's comment riotously funny, as did I.

Larry attended my first wedding. If he thought, as many did, I later learned, the marriage would be over in six months, he was kind enough not to share that prediction with me.

Not too long after establishing my life in L.A. before moving to Manhattan, I enrolled in acting classes in the highly regarded actors' studio in Hollywood called The Loft. The theater in The Loft was quite small, very dark, with some stage lighting, and seating for students and guests on tiered benches from floor to ceiling up one side of the space. The owners and teachers were Peggy Feury and Bill Traylor, a power couple in the world of training actors. Angelica Huston thanked Peggy in her acceptance speech at the Oscars when she won Best Actress for *Prizzi's Honor*. Angelica was just the tip of the iceberg.

Peggy was a brilliant and enigmatic person. She always sat in the same place while watching scenes performed by her students—at the far end of the bottom bench with her head resting against the wall. Peggy suffered from narcolepsy and often appeared to doze off during scene work, with her eyes closed, often through the entirety of the scene. She'd then wake up and fully critique performances, having missed not a single detail. In my four years as a student, several notable celebrities and actors came and went, such as Tina Turner, Sean Penn, Jeff Goldblum, and quite a few others.

I received a call at home one afternoon from a woman in Leo Penn's office, asking for me by name. She said that Mr. Penn was directing a TV series of *Little Women* for Paramount, and he would like me to read for the part of Jo March. Figuring it was a prank call, of course, I hung up. She called back. I asked if she was sure she had the right number. She asked if I was sure I was Jodi Mitchel. I said I was the last time I checked. She asked if I'd like to read for Mr. Penn or not. I said I would. We scheduled an appointment and I hung up the phone, wondering how on Earth this happened. I knew who Leo Penn was, but could not for my little life imagine how the hell he knew who I was, let alone have my number.

What I didn't put together was that Leo Penn was Sean's father. I later learned that after seeing my work in class on several occasions, Sean gave his dad my name and suggested he see me for the role of Jo. After the initial reading, I was brought in for two callbacks. I didn't get the part, but came pretty close. Of course close means absolutely nothing, but it was validating to reach that level on a major audition at that point in my career. Sean never let on, and neither did I.

Then there were the less-empowering auditions. In a beautiful office in Hollywood with sunlight streaming in through enormous windows, reflecting brightly off the many glass and chrome fixtures and furnishings, and gorgeous art and objects around the room, I was about to read for a major producer at 20th Century. This was my second big reading, and I was crazy anxious. The producer seemed like a nice guy, eager to put me at ease. He said, "I can tell you're nervous. Please don't be. I'll read with you. This is a romantic scene between the two main characters. Why don't we sit on the sofa?" He gave me the sides, described the project and the role, and we began reading.

Within three minutes of starting to read, he put his hand on my thigh.

I froze. He moved closer to me as his hand traveled further up my thigh. I stood up abruptly, nearly knocking over a huge floral arrangement in a gigantic vase, thanked him, and left the building. With smoke pouring out of my ears as I got in my car, I proceeded to cry, scream, and beat the shit out of the steering wheel, swirling in a toxic mix of rage, shame, embarrassment, and helplessness. It was my first—but would not be my last—rodeo on the casting couch. I knew my way around those emotions, but the assaults and insults never got easier to manage. Missed out on quite a few roles that way.

I spent my twenty-fifth birthday in an L.A. courtroom as Chuck E. Weiss, who I was dating, and Tom Waits, who we constantly hung out with, were facing charges of loitering in Las Vegas. Does anyone do anything *but* loiter in Las Vegas? I mean, isn't that what Las Vegas is for? The first night I walked the Strip, I was struck by the sight of hundreds of breasts desperately straining to escape the confines of dresses so tight that breathing seemed out of the question.

After an entire day in court, the charges against Weiss and Waits were dropped. It would be the first of two occasions I'd spend in an L.A. courtroom, the second defending myself.

I had an absolute ball dating Chuck E., hanging out with him and Tom at The Troubadour, L.A.'s dimmest-lit, smokiest, loudest, most crowded, coolest, and iconic club. Rickie Lee Jones performed there quite often, and when she did, the four of us would hang out well into the night.

Rickie Lee seemed somewhat intrigued by Chuck E.'s and my romance and wrote and recorded "Chuck E.'s in Love" while we were dating. There was widespread speculation about whether the song was about me, her, or Chuck E.'s distant cousin in Denver. Tom thought it was Denver, Chuck E. thought it was me, and Rickie Lee would never say. Watching Tom's and Rickie Lee's careers rising meteorically and being out and about with them and Chuck E., as they all became the stuff of L.A. legend, was heady stuff.

Tom and I had insomnia in common, as well as an appreciation for off-color jokes. We'd call each other in the wee hours to share our latest inappropriate but always hilarious witticisms. If I had to be awake all night suffering from monkey-mind, hearing Waits' signature voice on the other end of the phone was a welcome distraction.

Whoever was calling whom dispensed with the pleasantries, such as "Hi, it's Jodi," or "It's me, Waits," and immediately launched into the evening's story. When I had my tonsils removed at twenty-eight—no fun at that age—my mom came to care for me while I recovered. I was still in the hospital, due for discharge the following day, and my mother, asleep in my apartment, frantically picked up the phone when it rang at 3 a.m., thinking it was the hospital calling to say I was dead. It was Tom. Of course she didn't know that, assuming she'd answered a prank call. I never saw the need to enlighten her. Missing one of Waits' colorful installments was my only regret.

In honor of the occasion of my thirtieth birthday, I dropped thirty pounds in a way that could've landed me in the morgue—as could have many of the choices I was making in those days—and had all my hair cut off, leaving about two inches. At a birthday party I threw for myself at the Improv, weighing in at an anorexic one hundred thirteen pounds, in an off-the-shoulder dress revealing collarbones I never knew I had and haven't seen since, someone told me I looked like Audrey Hepburn. I thought, "I've never been nor will I ever be happier. I can die now." I'm still surprised I didn't.

In hindsight, I realize my dad and I had dueling compulsions around food. His was about controlling whatever he could, including how much my brothers and I ate and when. Mine stemmed from him monitoring the refrigerator every night after dinner. While reading voraciously, he would sit in the living room chair that gave him the clearest sightline to the fridge to ensure no one opened it at any point after dinner. "What're you doing in the refrigerator? You just had dinner!" Dinner was at 6:00. It was 9:00.

I came to understand that multiple significant weight losses throughout my adult life revealed my yearning to be something other than I was. Actually to disappear, if at all possible.

CHAPTER 12
A PRISONER CALLED WANDA

I told one of my closest friends in L.A. that I would soon be moving to New York. Unhappy with the news, she thought she could dissuade me by giving me a puppy. Quite manipulative, but it worked for a while. Sapphire, a small Keeshond/Norwegian ElkHound mix, was gorgeous, with bright blue eyes rimmed with thick, black lashes. She looked like Tony Curtis (Zac Efron, for you younger folk). When she was still little, some friends from high school, one living in L.A. and one in San Francisco, and I decided to spend Memorial Day weekend in the cool seaside town of Newport Beach. To celebrate the occasion, we'd each purchased a gram of cocaine.

Sharing a hotel room, we settled Sapphire out on the fully enclosed deck with her little bed, toys, food, and water and left to find a restaurant. After a lobster dinner, we headed to the beach to enjoy what was shaping up to be a beautiful night. Each of us had our little stash of cocaine in our purses, enjoying a joint after imbibing, and chilling on the gorgeous beach. Eileen took the last hit on the roach and put it out in the sand next to her.

As the three of us were enjoying the evening, a homeless guy stopped by, wanting to chat. He had long matted hair, wore a stained baseball cap, dirty clothing, and a torn Members Only jacket. We said as nicely as we could that we really didn't want to be bothered and would he mind leaving us alone so we could continue our conversation. He then removed his hat, which took his hair with it, flashed a badge, put his fingers in the sand in the exact spot where Eileen had doused the roach, and said he would be searching our purses. He found each packet of cocaine and informed us we were under arrest. We thought he was kidding.

Instructing us to stand up, he handcuffed us together and called for a police car. When it arrived, we were unable to get in. We were backward. Still cuffed together, we turned around, looking like the Rockettes, but with shorter legs. This little bit of choreography sent us off into gales of laughter. We were high, don't forget. Now facing forward, still cuffed, we awkwardly piled into the car. Our friend, the homeless cop, climbed into the passenger seat, and we were driven to a small local jail.

Once inside, the handcuffs were removed, and we were deposited into a cell. I was sneezing my head off, and Deidre was freaking out to the point that she threw up in the toilet inside the cell. We were instructed not to flush. We never found out why, but assumed they'd want to examine the contents of her stomach. What'd we know?

We were told we could each make a phone call and should try to arrange bail. It made sense for Eileen to make a call since her dad was an attorney. Neither Deidre nor I were about to call our parents and couldn't think of anyone else who could post bail. Eileen told her dad what happened and where we were. He said to sit tight. He'd take care of it. Nothin' like white privilege.

After several hours, a cop opened the cell, cuffed us again, and instructed us to follow him. We were ushered into another car, driven by a different cop, off into the darkness. Eileen, handcuffed to my left wrist, tapped me on the shoulder and slipped the cuff off her right wrist, quietly giggling as she did so. Replacing the handcuff just in time, we pulled up to a mammoth windowless structure in the night, eerily lit and looming over the landscape, looking exactly like what it was—a humongous women's prison. Believe me when I tell you, there's a world of difference between a jail and a prison, which we were about to learn in horrifying detail.

Turning off the engine, the cop looked back at us and said, "Listen to me, girls. You cannot fuck around in there. You must do exactly what you're told exactly when you're told to do it. Just follow instructions, and you'll be fine." And now it was official. We're scared out of our teeny tiny freaking little sheltered minds.

As we enter the building, bars open and close in front of and behind us, and the first thing we learn is why it's called "the slammer." Loud doesn't come close. Christ, *deafening* doesn't come close. We were ushered into a small room, and like a scene out of some dark, surreal Jean Cocteau film, a matron sitting at a desk at a window well above where we're standing, leans out, looks down, and says to someone we couldn't see, "There's no way these girls are twenty-one." Eileen is 4-foot-10, Deidre a couple of inches taller, and I'm 5-foot-4." She leans back out the window, looks down upon us, and says, "If you girls aren't minors, by the time you leave here, you'll wish you were." *What the fuck does that mean?* Then they took our belts and shoes. Were they expecting us to hang ourselves or gouge our eyes out with our heels?

In the next small room, another matron poked around in our hair, ran her latex-gloved fingers around the inside of our mouths, and led us into a holding tank full of women, a cinder block cell with no windows, a metal bench bolted to the wall around the perimeter, and a couple of toilets similarly secured.

We learned that on holiday weekends, they'd sweep the beaches, arresting people for all sorts of infractions. A very large woman was snoring louder than I knew anyone could snore, passed out on her back, teetering on the bench. Soon after our arrival, she fitfully awakened, swung her legs off the bench, struggled to sit up, looked around, and realizing where she was, again, slammed her fist into the wall so hard I was certain she'd broken it. She was a little irritated. Another girl sitting on the bench asked me a question I never expected to be asked in the entirety of my life, except when I starred in a movie. "What are you in for?" I told her and asked the same question. She was picked up for kiting checks. Seemed relatively harmless in the grand scheme of crime.

I was holding up okay after several hours, until I asked a matron what would happen if we couldn't arrange bail soon. She said we'd be taken up to housing.

"What happens in housing," I asked.

"You'll shower and change."

Shower?? *That can't be good*, thought this Jewish girl.

Deidre was starting to crack. Sitting on my lap weeping, she looked like a ventriloquist's dummy suffering a psychotic break. It got quite dramatic when she went to the bars, stuck her face between them, yelling as she wept, "We're being treated like common criminals." Clearly, it had not occurred to her that we *were* common criminals.

All smokers at the time, we would have gladly cut off almost any part of our body for a cigarette. After wailing to the wind through the bars, Deidre did a slow-motion slump to her knees. With her face where it began, her cheeks desperately trying to remain at their starting point, she sobbed all the way down, "All we want is a lousy cigarette!" It was a scene straight out of every women-behind-bars B-movie ever made.

Having overheard Deidre, which would have been hard not to do, one of our cell mates cheerfully asked if we'd like a cigarette. You would have thought she offered us each a gold brick. We said, "Oh my god. Yes please, oh please, oh my god, yes!" Reaching into a pocket in her little sweater, taking out a pack of cigarettes, she handed us each two, one for now and one for later. Slightly jarring to think there might be a later. We thanked her countless times as we waited for her to offer a light. Finally, Eileen asked if she had a match. She said, "Oh no. Smoking's not allowed." That sent Deidre right over the edge.

Soon we were taken to be fingerprinted and have our mugshots taken. We learned that the Empress of Cruelty, our tobacco dealer, was named Wanda. She wore a flouncy pink sparkly skirt and pink cardigan over a little white lacy blouse. Her platinum blonde hair with three inches of black roots stuck out in directions I never knew existed. She liked to pace around the holding tank, singing at the top of her lungs, "Hail! Hail! The gang's all here! What the hail do we care?!"

I was curious about Wanda and asked the cop fingerprinting me what she had done. He said, "She assaulted an officer with a deadly weapon."

"What was the weapon?" I asked.

"A car."

Floating bad checks to attempted vehicular homicide of a cop. Quite the spectrum of offenses.

After being returned to holding, we were finally, which had taken on a whole new meaning that night, informed that we were free to go. Eileen's father had arranged bail. Being a good little prisoner, I had decided it was wise to park my mouth for a while. But, as we collected our belongings from the matron at the window on the way out, and she gave me shit about something or other, my attitude came screeching back and leapt out.

I made some wisecrack. She asked if I'd like to return to holding. If so, she could arrange it. I nearly bit off the tip of my tongue.

Finding a payphone to call a taxi, we got back to Eileen's car and returned to the hotel. Sapphire, wading in two inches of puppy shit, was quite happy to see us. I cleaned up the deck, gave her a bath, we all took showers with no terrifying connotation, and ordered room service: cheeseburgers, fries, and three bottles of champagne.

Luckily, Eileen and I had a very close friend in L.A. who was an attorney, willing to discuss our case. Alton and his wife, Patti, were two of our closest friends, and with Deidre back in San Francisco, Eileen and I met with them in their home. Alton invited us into his large and lawyerly-looking study. He said, "We need to get something very important out of the way first." He seemed almost somber. Eileen and I looked at one another apprehensively, wondering what the hell this was about.

Alton closed the drapes across the wide expanse of windows, sat down at his large mahogany desk, and pulled something from the drawer. It was a ten-inch square mirror lined with cocaine. As I write this, it seems appalling. At the time, it was very funny and much welcomed. Ah, the '80s!

A court date was set in downtown L.A. At the end of a full day, Eileen and Deidre received probation with a requirement to see drug counselors. The charges against me were dropped. Since the undercover cop had no probable cause to search my purse, the cocaine was inadmissible. A happy outcome for me, without question. But my great good fortune in it all was the acquisition of a fabulous story to tell. You know I love a good story!

CHAPTER 13
I EXCELLED AT GETTING FIRED

Growing up pissed off, acutely resenting the forces in control, I developed a highly evolved disdain for authority, rules, and hearing "No." I despise the word, unless I ask, "Do I have cancer?" "No, you can't," causes a markedly unpleasant reaction in me. My temperature spikes, my cheeks itch, my ears ring, and my thinking becomes slightly impaired. Not surprisingly, I struggle with impulse control and unleash occasional snark attacks. This might explain my eight-page resume.

The question was: How many jobs would it take until I was able to keep one? My first job interview was for a teller-in-training at a bank in Beverly Hills. Without a car, I had to take two buses each way. Excited for my interview, I donned my "you might not realize it, but I'm the ideal employee" outfit—a little black shirtwaist with white polka dots, three-quarter sleeves with white turned-up cuffs, a white Peter Pan collar with a dainty black bow at the throat, and a wide black patent leather belt. I put on my black-and-white patent leather stacked heels and carried my little black patent leather purse. The dress was on the short side. I wish to God I had a photograph. Did I look professional? Ridiculous? Adorable? Laughable? I have no idea, but I got the job.

To illustrate exactly how professional I was, I showed up for my first day of training chewing gum. Ten of us were assembled at tables arranged in a U shape in a large conference room under harsh fluorescent lights, with the instructor inside the U. She walked over to me, continuing to speak to the class while she walked, and, still speaking, put her hand under my chin. She never stopped talking, but made it clear I was to spit out my gum. Maybe she had previously been a third-grade teacher, or mistook me for a third-grade student. My thought was, *Should be fun telling the folks I got fired from my first job in the first half of my first day.* Who knows why, but I wasn't fired. Yet.

On my first day of work following training, I made another wise decision—to wear a cute little blouse, my black and white patent leather shoes, and a cut-off blue jean skirt, shorter than my shirtwaist. My supervisor quietly told me to go home and change. Starting to itch, I said, "I don't have a car. I take two buses here and two buses home," to which she replied, "Then I guess you'd better get going."

Barely hearing her over the ringing in my ears, I argued that it hardly made sense for me to go home and come back. I'd get back just in time to leave again. "In that case," she said, "you can leave, and you don't need to come back."

Next was a job as a switchboard operator for an answering service called Courtesy Voices. The owner was Miss Curtis. I always thought it should be spelled Curtis-y Voices. This was, even in the '80s, an antiquated plug-in switchboard with a line of women seated down the row on both sides of the room, like you've seen in a million '40s movies. Answering phones for doctors' offices, legal practices, small businesses, private residences, etc., we were all instructed to identify ourselves as Miss Curtis.

Picking up a call for a doctor's office, I answered in a lilting voice, "Dr. Brown's office. Miss Curtis speaking. May I help you?"

There was a pause on the other end. The caller hesitantly asked, "Is this a recording?"

It was irresistible. I had no choice. What would you have done? I said, "Yes," and heard the caller's brain collapse just before she hung up.

Unbeknownst to me, the real Miss Curtis listened in on calls from time to time. Of course, she was listening in on this one. She informed me that my services were no longer needed.

A slew of waitressing jobs ended similarly, including my first, when I was living in Manhattan. In an upscale, tiny Italian restaurant on my first night on the job, I walked past a table where a couple was enjoying their appetizers. As I passed, one of them accidentally brushed their dinner fork off the table to the floor. Eager to be immediately and ever-so-helpful, I enthusiastically picked it up and placed it back on the table. The maître d', observing my quick thinking and impressive customer service skills, took me aside and told me I could hang up my apron and leave. I did not need to return.

My first waitressing job in L.A. was in Marina del Rey at a seafood restaurant with a nautical theme. My uniform was a little—and I do mean *little*—one-piece red, white, and blue number with a skirt, if you can call it that, barely covering my ass. The bodice had a lace-up, plunging neckline required by management to be left loosely tied. Putting the uniform on for my first shift, I asked the manager if there might be something else I could wear. She told me this was probably not the restaurant for me, and I could go.

My next adventure in culinary service was at Mark Twain's Notorious Jumping Frog Saloon, a new establishment in deluxe Brentwood. The decor was turn-of-the-century, with waitresses in long skirts and high-collared blouses in the Gibson Girl look. I flat-out lied to get this job. It was all tray service, which I had never done but said I had. Meals were delivered on heavy porcelain dishes with hefty metal plate covers on large oval trays we were required to carry one-handed. Touching the tray with your other hand was forbidden, except when placing it on the tray stand.

My parents were visiting on my first night and came in for dinner. They were quite entertained, watching my comings and goings. Serving my very first customers at the Saloon, I was carrying an absurdly heavy tray with six meals piled in three stacks, when I tripped over my fucking skirt. The tray crashed on the hardwood floor in the loudest disaster I'd heard in my young life, as steaks and lobster and fish and pasta and salads and sides and porcelain dishes and metal dish covers slid in all directions. Management was kind enough to allow me to serve my parents, then leave with them when they finished their meal. No dessert.

Then there was the bar/restaurant that stayed open until 2 a.m. I was closing when a couple came in at 1:30 for pastries and coffee. I was livid. I went back to the kitchen and mouthed off to the manager. "How stupid is it to keep this restaurant open for two customers whose order will barely cover the cost of the electricity to heat their coffee?" After serving the couple, the manager informed me that she had spoken with the owner.

They decided that since I was the most dispensable person on staff, they'd dispense with me. Direct quote.

The owner of a restaurant in New York with a black-and-white tile floor told me at the end of a double shift—during which I'd sat down once, and that was on the toilet—that he couldn't stand the sound of my heels on the floor and that I didn't need to come back.

And then, I finally landed the gig at the Improv. To illustrate just how successful I was at losing jobs, I'll tell you that in my tenure at the Improv, I was fired on four separate occasions for various infractions. The first was running after a customer on the street who'd failed to tip me on a sizable tab. I asked if he understood I wasn't "jerking off in there, but trying to make a living." Word got back to Bud, the owner. I was fired. And rehired several days later.

Then, a fairly famous actor asked for whipped cream to put on the cheesecake I'd baked and sold to the club. (Songbird Cheesecake is insanely good. Another talent acquired from Paula Ruth. I've had multiple proposals of marriage after one bite.)

When this guy asked for whipped cream, I, of course, questioned why he wanted it. He looked at me as if to say, what the hell business is it of yours and said it was for his cheesecake. I said, "I'm sorry. You're not putting whipped cream on my cheesecake." It had a sour cream topping for Chrissakes! Whipped cream? Absolutely not. Word got back to Bud. I was fired. And rehired several days later.

The third was when I spilled an entire plate of food—a huge cheese-burger, a mountain of fries, and two little cups of ketchup—between a customer and the back of his chair as he leaned forward watching Jay Leno. I whispered to him not to sit back. I'll be back in a jiff. Word got back to Bud. I was fired. And rehired several days later.

The fourth incident was the result of my own flabbergasting stupidity. I wanted to call in sick one night, but couldn't come up with an excuse. Then, I had what I thought was a stroke of genius. I called and said I broke my finger. Problem was, I hadn't really thought it through. Nothing new. I had to return to work with a splint on my finger, which slowed my delivery quite a bit. Word got back to Bud. You know. But since he wanted to sleep with me, I was forgiven each time. Hope springs eternal in the lecherous heart. May I say his prurient little wish never materialized. Ew.

CHAPTER 14
NICK EDEN

Responding to an audition notice in *Variety*, I drove my spiffy new used first-car-I-ever-owned Volkswagen hatchback I'd purchased for six hundred dollars to the Valley. I loved that car. Probably not one of my better decisions, though, as it was a stick shift, which I'd never driven. Why would I buy a car I had no idea how to drive? Optimism. Perhaps misplaced. After sideswiping a parked bus, which accordioned the passenger door, and rear-ending a dump truck, mangling the front end, not on the same day, I sold the car. It fetched a stunning twenty-five dollars.

Back in the Valley, the gentleman holding the audition in his sparsely furnished, slightly dingy apartment informed another young woman and me that he was a club singer looking to hire two attractive sidekicks for his new club act to be called "Nick Eden and his Foxy Ladies." That right there should've sent me screaming into the street.

Nick had no piano, so Carolyn and I sang *a cappella*. She was a mediocre singer, but that didn't matter to Nick. Much more important was that she could make our costumes. And she was blonde. He hired us both.

A couple of weeks into rehearsals, he took us to Knott's Berry Farm, a Western-themed amusement park. I wondered why. Silly me! To take our promo photos in their free Pitcher Gallery, of course (and no, that's not a typo). You could have your photo snapped on a stuffed life-sized rearing horse, or stick your head in the holes of cardboard cutouts, where the faces of cartoonish saloon singers and cowboys and bartenders and all manner of dusty Western characters should have been, and go home with a really great pitcher.

It was high noon on a sweltering August day. Cue the theme song to *The Good, The Bad, and The Ugly.* Nick was The Bad *and* The Ugly. He was in his best (read pathetic) Rat Pack finery. Carolyn and I went into the jammed public restroom with an inch of slime on the floor to change into our almost-satin-but-really-polyester floor-length gowns with rhinestone spaghetti straps and glittery sandals with seven-inch heels.

Sporting a full face of theatrical makeup, including ridiculously long false eyelashes, I was perspiring like a little pig and looked a bit oily. The heat and humidity had tightened my curls into dark brown fusilli. I looked like a sweaty brunette Harpo. I'm not sure that was the look Nick was going for, but that's all I had. Carolyn and I stood back-to-back in front of a blank backdrop with our hands on our hips, looking—at Nick's direction—as sultry as possible. Sultry? Maybe. Clammy? Got it.

With photos and costumes at the ready, it was time for our first performance in the Inca Room at the La Mirada Bowl. Nick continually insisted that this would be a "class act all the way." I think it's safe to say the Inca Room at the La Mirada Bowl was the classiest Inca Room in any bowling alley anywhere.

Upon entering the small Inca Room, with nary a window, patrons were treated to the sight of a few tiki torches scattered around, lots of spray-painted shiny gold and silver surfaces, plenty of fake foliage and plastic vines, an inflatable cactus in one corner and a DIY totem pole in another. A "stage" had been built on one side of the room, all of six inches high. In the middle of the stage sat a mic stand and barstool. On the opposite wall was a spotlight Nick had rented, designed for a one-thousand-seat theater. Once you were in the spot, you were functionally blind... for a while.

Perched on that stool with Carolyn and me on either side, Nick, the worst Sinatra impersonator you ever saw, performed his very best renditions of "My Way," "New York, New York," and "Strangers in the Night," while Carolyn and I offered our finest, most melodious "*oooohhs*" and "*aaahhhhs*," sung, at Nick's direction, as seductively as possible. The most people in the bar at any time during any show was seven, including the bartender.

You may have surmised that I'm no shrinking violet. I'm not easily offended or flushed. But I have to say, Nick Eden had the foulest mouth I'd ever heard and told the filthiest jokes imaginable. And to make it all that much worse, he was decked out in a shiny suit, slightly discolored white ruffled shirt with too many buttons open, a profoundly cliched untied bow tie hanging around his neck, a too-tight cummerbund around his paunchy middle, with an ever-present cigarette dangling from lips so thin they were nearly fictional.

After a week of performances, as the last show ended, Nick informed Carolyn and me that he wouldn't be able to pay us for a while. I politely queried, "You're fucking kidding, right?" He offered some lame excuse, which sent me storming out of the Inca Room into the blinding lights of the La Mirada Bowl, where a gigantic poster hanging over Lane Six caught my squinting eyes. It featured a graphic of two huge bowling balls and read *"You'll Strike All Night With Ed Spitalnick's Balls. Spitalnick's. Best Balls In The Alley."* And that made the entire sordid affair of my first job in showbiz—with the smarmiest, least talented performer alive at the time—worth every humiliating moment.

CHAPTER 15
POOR CHOICE OF A HUSBAND 1.0

I didn't start getting married until I was thirty-one. I was busy getting high, laid, and fired. Enter Joe. A short, Italian version of my dad, absent the redeeming value. A cute, talented, funny, seemingly sweet guy who was a songwriter and performer. And potentially my first shot at that sperm donor. It's possible my vision was a bit blurry, not seeing Joe for what he was, as I was a tad desperate. Per "The Decision," I am now three years behind schedule.

Joe and I met and moved in together in short order. We were quite taken with one another and decided to get married five months after starting to date. While home in Pittsburgh, I showed his headshot to my brothers and parents as we all sat around the living room, and announced that I was getting married. Ira, lying on the floor, took a look at the picture, handed it back to me, and said with not a hint of concern, "He's a maniac." How did he know?

It was fun for a while. We ran in the same circles and had many mutual friends in the music industry: managers, musicians, writers, performers, etc. Joe was a great singer and keyboardist. I went to all his gigs, and we attended performances of our other musician friends. We spent time in the comedy clubs and had great fun. I went to Milwaukee with him to meet his mom, sister, and brother. Wonderful people. Joe's mom played a mean stride piano. It was evident where his talent came from. They all embraced me, making me feel welcome in the family.

A few months after moving in together, things started to head south. Our relationship began to resemble mine with my father. Joe was excessively controlling, with a hair-trigger temper. He had plenty to say about what I wore, how I styled my hair, what I ate, and when he thought I was gaining weight.

In a notably ugly argument, sometime after he proposed and the wedding was planned, he kept menacingly poking me in the chest while screaming at me. He backed me into a wall. Feeling terrified and trapped, I told him he was frightening me and asked him to please lower his voice and back up. He brought his face as close as he could to mine and kept screaming and poking. I ran around him into a closet and slammed the door, relieved I was able to lock it from the inside. I sat trembling on the floor in the dark in as tight a ball as my body could curl into, not realizing the closet was the new dining room hutch.

Like those under-the-hutch moments when no one cared to look for me, Joe never came to see if I was okay after I had been in there for some time. I was finally able to pull myself together and leave the closet. Knowing it would trigger him, it took a while to work up the courage to suggest that we put the wedding off, since we seemed to be fighting a lot. There was nothing to discuss, he insisted. We were going through with it. We'd already sent out the invitations. Oh. Well then. Clearly, I had not yet developed the fine art of self-determination and acquiesced.

Needing to get away, I went to New York and stayed with Ava. Time away provided a welcome break from the tension at home. I was in deep denial of just how much control I had handed over to Joe. Speaking to him on the phone several times a day, I reported in almost every conversation what I had eaten that day, assuring him I'd consumed very little sugar and hadn't gained any weight. Overhearing several of these conversations, Ava became concerned and sat me down for what was a difficult and painful conversation.

My neural synapses were clearly misfiring. Otherwise, I would've understood that Joe, a confessed recovering bulimic, was projecting onto me his deep-rooted food and body image obsessions, which I sure as hell didn't need, as I had plenty of my own. Of course, had I been in good mental and emotional health, I would not have made many of the choices

I was making. Remaining in a relationship with Joe, not to mention marrying him, highlighted in flashing neon the degree of self-punishment I was inflicting.

Our honeymoon in Santa Barbara made it clear that my husband did not want to be married. It took some high-level deductive reasoning skills to figure that one out. His disappearance for six hours on our wedding night was my first big clue. I spent a beautiful, balmy evening sitting alone on the balcony of our gorgeous hotel room under a sky glittering above me where diamonds stood in for stars, listening to what should have been the mesmerizing sound of the water below, but was instead deeply depressing. When Joe finally materialized, I asked where he had been. He mumbled something, undressed, washed up, got into bed, and went to sleep. The next six months were a lot of fun.

We began couples counseling soon after returning home. Joe was finally able to say he didn't want to be married. Really? I coulda toldja that, pal. A summary dissolution, thankfully easy to obtain, landed my first marriage squarely in the annals of Jodi Mitchel's Less-Than-Illustrious Marital History. I later learned odds were placed at the wedding on how long the marriage would last. My parents won the bet.

Hearing about the divorce, my mom swore if she knew how to drive a truck, she'd run him over, back up across his limp body, and do it again. Now *that's* love.

Let's take stock, shall we? Not only am I divorced at thirty-three, but there are no romantic prospects in sight, nor any kids in the foreseeable future. And I'm five years behind the 8-ball. I took a minute to regroup, eventually realizing I had dodged yet another bullet. Well, not dodged, exactly. I was grazed.

With ever-rising feelings of pessimism, hopelessness, anxiety, and plummeting self-esteem, I struggled to come to grips with a failed marriage, my age, childlessness, and soon-to-be-waning fertility. Fortunately, my trusty superhero, Fightin' Little Jodi, came thundering in, shouting, "Get up, Jode. We got work to do! Tick fucking tock!!"

CHAPTER 16

MR. WRONG 2.0/
PERFECT KID 1.0

And then came Dean.

Perhaps you've heard the stunningly beautiful song "The Rose," written by Amanda McBroom. Amanda and her talented husband, George Ball, are close and wonderful friends. I had not yet met Amanda when George and I were performing at the Improv in L.A. in a musical of Harry Chapin's music called *Taxi*.

George had the most gorgeous baritone I ever heard and was just the sweetest guy. I loved working with him. During a break in rehearsal one afternoon, he asked me to listen to the lyrics of a song his wife was in the midst of writing. Blown away, I told George they were the most beautiful lyrics I'd ever heard. Later listening to the lyrics of "The Rose" put to Amanda's exquisite music, it was evident she was a gigantic talent.

Meanwhile, Ava was now living in L.A. She and I grew up singing and harmonizing through our school years. We continued singing together at every opportunity well into adulthood. So when Amanda asked Ava and me to sing backup for her when "The Rose" was first performed on national TV, we were thrilled. Not only is Amanda a gifted songwriter, but she possesses one of the purest and most exquisite voices you've ever heard. She and I went on to do a lot of musical work together, including demo productions of several musicals she wrote and was shopping to producers.

Amanda and I sang backup for David Soul. If you're old enough, you might remember the very popular TV series *Starsky and Hutch*. David Soul was Hutch, or "The Blonde," as he was known. He was a singer and actor with a hit song entitled *"Don't Give Up On Us, Baby."* Capitalizing on the success of his hit, he put a band together and mounted an extensive tour.

Amanda and I toured Japan with David twice, as well as other countries, and had an absolute ball. She was unavailable when David put his third tour together, and Ava took over for her. David very generously gave us a solo. We sang one of Tom Wait's most beautiful songs, "I Wish I Was In New Orleans," and were overwhelmed by the audience reaction. It became one of the highlights of David's show. We toured Canada, the entire UK, and filmed a TV show in Monte Carlo with Cher, Petula Clark, and Aretha Franklin on the bill. Yes, *that* Aretha, as if there were any other!

I was breathless at the idea of meeting her, let alone hearing her sing live. We were all backstage waiting for our spots, where Aretha was splendiferous in a full-length white mink with an enormous stand-up collar, which she clutched tightly around her neck to keep her vocal cords warm. As she sipped the hot tea with lemon that she was never without before, in between and after performances, I found the courage to approach her and said, "Ms. Franklin,"—I was in the presence of nobility, after all—"I am a huge admirer and wanted to tell you how much I love your music." She silently smiled, put her hand out for me to take—which I did, feeling bewitched. She then floated away, an apparition in white, went on stage, and blew the roof off.

Amanda asked me to sing on a demo for a guy who had written a musical he wanted to pitch to producers. I said I'd be happy to. I met Dean and his partner, Harvey, at Amanda and George's house for the recording of songs from their musical, *Hamelin*.

A Jack Kerouac type, Dean was intriguing—a world away from what I was used to—and, therefore, quite attractive. He wore only black clothing, including an ever-present hat, all of which he described as made from petroleum byproducts. He had a quirky sense of humor, a unique worldview, and an idiosyncratic style. It didn't take long. I was bewitched.

He also seemed broken, somehow. I knew a little something about broken men, but clearly not much about my attraction to them. I hadn't yet come to understand that their allure had much to do with my need to fix them, stemming from my desperate desire to repair my dad those many years ago. Getting to know Dean better, I learned of a gigantic commitment phobia acquired from witnessing several of the many marriages between his parents. I later learned more.

Dean and I dated for some time. I just loved how different he was from any guy I'd ever been with. He was fun and funny, talented, sweet, and whip-smart. *Hamelin* had been picked up for production and mounted in a very cool, tiny club in L.A. called The Olio. I was cast in the role of Gertrude, the wife of the mayor of Hamelin. It was a great part. Gertrude was the brains behind the power—ruthless, diabolical, and very funny. The show had a successful run at The Olio, receiving wonderful reviews.

After the show on Saturdays, the cast, along with Dean and Harvey, would perform for folks from the audience who'd hang around, as well as other performers and friends who'd come by. We'd sing in a cabaret club format well into the night. It was the most fun and fulfilling experience of my professional life to date.

After the success at The Olio, Dean and Harvey landed a producer in New York. *Hamelin* would be mounted at the Circle in the Square, one of New York's premier off-Broadway theaters. Some of the L.A. cast would transition to New York, and other roles would be recast.

Dean and I moved to Princeton, New Jersey, into a small rental house an hour from NYC, to cast, rehearse, and mount the show. What was a charming, quirky little show in a funky, hole-in-the-wall venue in L.A. did not translate to the New York theater scene, and was, unfortunately, painfully panned. Every single performer was skewered by every paper, but not a single word was written about my performance in any review. I considered it a collection of raves.

After the show closed, I established a successful voiceover career in Philadelphia, while Dean wrote music and poetry, and performed in various venues. Life was fairly sweet.

Along the way, I learned that Dean grew up with alcoholic parents. His father died of an alcohol-related illness when Dean was five years old. He told me that by the age of seven, it was clear he could rely on no one but himself. Dean came to this hard realization after coming home from elementary school on several occasions to find his mother in a deep sleep on the couch. He'd help her into bed, take care of himself and his younger brother for the afternoon and evening, and get them off to school in the morning. No big surprise that the very heavy burden of that degree of responsibility for himself and his little brother—not to mention the effects of feeling that he could not rely on dependable parenting—at such a young age would leave a mark.

Dean knew his father had been married several times before marrying his mom, and she once before they were married. After his dad died, his mother married at least two more times. Suffice to say, and understandably, Dean was not big on getting hitched.

As we know, I possessed that particularly useless characteristic of wanting to save men and change them into something they were constitutionally incapable of or steadfastly unwilling to become. But I'm nothing if not persuasive and succeeded in cajoling Dean into marrying me. If you ever need to convince someone to eat a bag of glass while standing in a razor-blade blizzard, I'm your gal.

Shortly after *Hamelin* closed during Christmas, we were staying with Dean's step-brother, Ray, and his wife, Connie, when Dean's mother died. She had been quite ill, and her death was not unexpected. The surprise came in the form of a phone call the next day.

Dean, Ray, and Connie were going out, and Connie asked me to pick up calls, so I answered the phone when it rang. A man asked for Dean. I explained he was not there, but I was his fiancé and offered to take a message. He identified himself as Dean's mother's attorney and in what seemed an enormous breach of appropriate legal conduct, informed me that Dean and his brother would equally share their mother's estate, which was quite sizable. I actually dropped the phone. Managing to pick it up, I put it to my ear, and choked out the words, "Thank you, I'll give him the message."

Dean never shared with me that his mother had money. As far as I knew, he was a pauper who made enough with his poetry, music, and performing to get by. So this news came as a bit of a seismic freaking shock. As soon as I hung up the phone, I went into the bathroom and, let's just say, blew my guts out. And I don't mean that I shot myself in the stomach. An instantaneous and extreme physical reaction overtook my body. I'd never experienced anything like it.

When Dean returned, I took him upstairs into the bedroom, closed the door, and tried to tell him what I'd learned. I was weeping. With joy. Not for myself, mind you, because I had not yet considered what his inheritance might mean to me. I was weeping for Dean, that he could pursue his poetry and music for as long as he wanted, without ever having to worry about making a living. I couldn't imagine what that must feel like and mean to him. It just seemed miraculous to me.

Knowing this would happen one day, Dean took it all in stride. I, however, was nonplussed. I grew up in a modest family and home with very little in the way of financial resources, so to me, the idea of financial stability and freedom was mind-blowing. When I allowed myself to contemplate what that would feel like, it really was hard to imagine. And it took me quite a while to come to terms with it all.

Dean and I were soon married. Twice. Once in Vermont by a justice of the peace with Ira and Mary present, and again in Pittsburgh by a rabbi in his temple with Gershon and my parents in attendance. Dean bought a beautiful home on seven acres in a gorgeous rural area in New Jersey by the last covered bridge left standing in the state. We settled into a life I would never have imagined I'd be living. It was nothing to which I'd ever aspired nor conjured in my wildest imaginings.

Remember my pony dream? Well, it came true for a few hours! A neighbor had horses and knew of my great love for them. He rode one of his horses to the house one afternoon and asked if I wanted to take him for a spin. I rode this beautiful creature for several hours with plenty of room to wander and run. My riding lessons many decades ago paid off and I couldn't wait to tell my dad. I was ecstatic.

CHAPTER 17
MANNY MARASCHINI

Dean and I were exceedingly fortunate to get pregnant soon after starting to try. *Pregnant! FINALLY!!* And oh! How I loved it! Not a smidge of morning sickness, but I was quite tired in the first trimester. Then some cosmic midwife flipped a switch on the first day of my second trimester and turned me into Wonder Woman. Positively fantastic.

With tremendous energy, enthusiasm, and optimism, I felt like I could do this ten more times, at least, and was exceedingly encouraged about the future prospects for my gaggle. I may be late to the party that was originally scheduled seven years earlier, I thought, but I was drop-dead certain I could make good on my repurposed Manhattan Project—one I was confident would bring much more joy to the world than the original.

I soon discovered the sheer vastness of the difference between being pregnant and giving birth. Like the difference between life in Valhalla as a mighty and magnificent empress, adorned with jewels and dripping in adoration—and life in a dungeon in the deepest recesses of hell, chained to a wall with lots of other tortured souls who hadn't showered in three thousand years. Let's just say that pregnancy is fun and delivery is not.

I gave birth to Charlie at thirty-five. He wasn't thirty-five—I was. He brought with him much gorgeousness and abundant perfection! Fingers, toes, ears, nose, all in their rightful place. I was euphoric since I was now seven years off the Manhattan mark, and a bit of the gaggle pressure had lifted.

We called him "Manny Maraschini: The Boy with the Cherry Chin"—a little silly song I sang to him... well... constantly, because it made him smile. And when he smiled, it looked like a tiny cherry was embedded in his wee chin.

He was simply the most astonishing thing of any sort I'd ever seen. The most wondrous, mystifying, mesmerizing confection of delight that ever lived. When I laid either eye on him, I could hardly stand it. And when I looked at him with both eyes—which was what I usually did, doubling the emotional whammy—the beauty of him was all but unbearable.

To think I created this creature—and that he nearly killed me upon arrival—was all just way too much.

I was euphoric and exhausted beyond reckoning. Beyond the capacity for rational thought. And obsessive worry was starting to rise. At a follow-up appointment with my midwife, I confessed I wasn't sleeping. The baby monitor was next to my bed, as I compulsively needed to hear every breath. Instructing me to turn off the monitor and get some rest, she said I needed to trust that Charlie would be fine and I was capable of keeping him safe.

What she didn't know was that *deeply-dumb-new-mother-me* had purchased a lambswool mattress cover for Charlie's crib. By turning off the monitor that first and only night, I was able to sleep until God knows what time. I snapped awake in terror, flipped on the monitor, and could hear Charlie breathing hard. Flying down the hall without a single toe touching the floor and bursting into his room, I found him beet red and soaking wet, with little bits of lambswool stuck to his sopping wet face. He was in warm pajamas and terribly overheated. I lifted him off the lambswool and removed his soaked PJs. He soon cooled down, his breathing slowed, and within a few minutes, he was fine. I was not.

The dimension of my shame, guilt, and fear was insurmountable. Days later, it started.

The floodgates opened, and the tears flowed. Rivers. For weeks. What the hell was this? Soon, the hallucinations began. Cinematic and horrifying. I walked into the den and "saw" Charlie hanging by his neck from the ceiling fan. Dead, of course.

In the nursery, I had one in high definition of Charlie asleep in his crib as his stuffed elephant spontaneously combusted, engulfing him in flames. He died, of course.

Another one had me in the dining room holding Charlie against my chest when a single shot rang out, piercing the window, striking him in the back. He was killed instantly.

I'd heard of postpartum depression, but never anything like this, and I was certain I was losing my mind. The overarching dread of it all was that I was a dangerously incompetent mother, incapable of keeping my child alive, certain that soon he'd be taken from me.

Turning to the wisest, most unflappable person I knew, I called Paula Ruth. Something was terribly wrong with me, I told her. She needed to come immediately. I have no recollection of how she got from Pittsburgh to New Jersey or how quickly she arrived. I only know she saved my life.

My mom sat with me. She laid with me. Walked with me. She let me cry. She held me. She sang to me the way she did when I was little, when she'd put me to bed. She stroked my hair in that rhythmic way, lightly brushing her hand across my ear, making the most primal and centering sound. She assured me it was going to be alright, and I was not sick or insane.

One afternoon she said, "We need to get you out of this house. Let's go to the Stockton Inn for lunch. Grab Charlie and bring the Snugli." The server brought hard rolls and butter to the table and we ordered strawberry margaritas. Neither of us were drinkers. My mom had one. I had three.

Charlie slept in the Snugli against my chest while we munched on crunchy rolls and drank. And laughed our asses off. My mother was simply the funniest person alive. At one point, I looked down to see Charlie's entire slumbering head covered in breadcrumbs. He was wearing a crust hat. That sent us off into peals of uncontrollable, loud hysterics, and we decided it was time to go. My mother called it a hooker's lunch: bread and booze.

Fortunately, she could drive, and we made it home in three pieces. I nursed Charlie and put him down. He slept for ten hours. Alcohol in breast milk will do that to a kid. And I slept, too. Deeply and for more consecutive hours than I had since he'd been born. My mother was my therapist, my nurse, my doula, enabling me to rest and recover. And, in so doing, rescued me. Three weeks after her arrival, I was able to let her go and raise my son.

Finally, after a nine-year delay, I made my first entry in the first column, and the first gosling was in the gaggle. Encouraged, I felt real hope that the remaining gaggle was on its way. My marriage, however, was on its way out.

While Dean had been a loving, devoted, and wonderful dad, our marriage was far from perfect. A difficult, unhappy, and unfulfilling marriage is what it was. And I had known it for some time. I just could not contemplate divorce number two at the age of thirty-eight. It was one thing to divorce with no children, but the thought of divorcing the father of my child was incredibly painful. Still, we were simply wrong for one another. I needed much more than he could give, and he needed me to need much less.

During an argument, Dean told me with curdling contempt that I'd turned into a Jewish mother. Second time I'd heard that. But this time, since I'm Jewish and had recently given birth, it was an astute observation. I was thrilled by my evolution. Dean was revolted. After six years together, a brief stint in couples counseling, and an ever-deteriorating quality of life, I spent approximately four minutes one day pondering whether I could remain in the marriage for financial stability.

Simply by virtue of the fact that I was having this internal conversation, I knew it was over. It became clear I'd made the right decision when Dean bitterly accused me of being unwilling to be unhappy. He had that part right. But how sad was it, and how many volumes did it speak, that he was?

CHAPTER 18
DIVORCE 2.0
SLIGHTLY MORE COMPLICATED THAN 1.0

With my beloved Charlie amongst the living and literate, I will not share much detail about how his father and I managed to extricate our lives from one another's. Suffice to say, it wasn't pretty and took forever. What made it particularly tricky was that we both continued to live in the house. I moved into another bedroom. I couldn't eat and wasn't sleeping. It was messy.

Working hard with our respective attorneys to come to fair and equitable terms that best served Charlie, it appeared at one point we might emerge from the divorce able to amicably coparent. That, to my profound disappointment, was not the case.

But finally, it was over, and with my nearly four-year-old Charlie, I moved back to Princeton. Dean and I agreed to shared custody, with Charlie spending a week at a time with each of us. It was like executing military maneuvers, but we made it work.

If you're keeping track, I'm now thirty-eight and twice-divorced. I have the perfect child, but hardly the gaggle I'd envisioned ten years earlier. And fertility was rapidly receding in the rearview.

CHAPTER 19
HUSBAND 3.0
NEARLY-PERFECT HUSBAND 1.0

The *Princeton Packet*, the local paper, did a feature in one of their June weekend editions when thoughts of the young-and-in-love turn to nuptials. The piece was about people who met at weddings and went on to date or get married. Jay, my third and final husband, and I were featured in the piece and landed on the cover of the section because not only had we met at a wedding ... we met at *my* wedding.

Actually, it was at the rehearsal dinner the night before my first wedding.

Joe and I hosted an informal gathering for out-of-town family and friends at the Gardenia, a great little L.A. club. Wanting to do something different, we put together a cabaret act. A friend of mine at the time and Jay's friend were living and dating in New York and would attend the wedding. She mentioned that her boyfriend's best friend was living in L.A. and asked if, since they'd only be in town for the wedding, he could come with them to our rehearsal dinner, which was really an informal get-together for family and out-of-town guests. I said of course.

The Gardenia was a long, narrow club with the entrance at one end, tables against the walls on either side, and a stage with a baby grand piano at the other end. I remember, in vivid detail, as Joe and I were onstage preparing for our show to begin, seeing an incredibly good-looking guy who I didn't know come into the club at the far end of the room. I wondered, *Holy shit! Who is that?* Figuratively slapping myself across the face, my next thought was, *What the hell does it matter who that is? You're getting married tomorrow!*

That guy was Jay. After Joe and I divorced and Dean and I were married, he and I slowly became friends. Dean and I hosted wedding and fortieth birthday parties for Jay's and my New York friends, both of which he attended.

Jay organized and conducted an annual fundraiser for muscular dystrophy every Labor Day weekend on the South Shore of Boston, where his family and many friends volunteered. Jerry Lewis was Jay's hero, not just for his comedic genius, which was pretty potent for a person like Jay aspiring to become a comedian, but for Lewis's selfless dedication to helping kids with muscular dystrophy. That began what is now a forty-eight-year tradition for Jay, which has raised over seven hundred fifty thousand dollars for the Muscular Dystrophy Association.

I started traveling to Boston to help with the event. Getting to know Jay, I discovered a kind, empathetic, genuine guy who was sweet, so funny, and someone I wanted to get to know better. In the throes of my divorce from Dean, I turned to Jay for a strong shoulder. He was one of the best listeners I knew, offering a steady hand and guidance through the emotional upheaval. I hoped he could be helpful in navigating the choppy waters. And he was.

With my divorce finalized in June, Charlie and I moved into our lovely new home on a beautiful tree-lined street in the Riverside neighborhood of Princeton—within walking distance of the synagogue we joined and Riverside Elementary School, which Charlie would attend for the next six years. There was a large front yard and a wonderful fenced-in backyard for Shirley, our funny-looking and beloved Scottish Deerhound. We settled in pretty effortlessly.

Soon after making the move, I thought it would be fun for Charlie if we added a kitten to our little family. An adorable and slightly manic black, white, and brown Tabby named Mickey soon moved in, and he and Shirley quickly fell in love. Charlie went back and forth between our homes every Monday when either Dean or I would pick him up after school for his week with each of us. It was in no way easy for Charlie but gave him ample time with both parents, something that was extremely important for him, and that I was very glad about.

And I continued to talk to Jay. Labor Day weekend, a year and a half after Dean and I divorced, when Charlie was with his father, I went to Boston to help with the fundraiser... with an ulterior motive.

Jay's event was a twenty-four-hour party held at the community center in his hometown, coinciding with the national Jerry Lewis telethon. His tradition was to rent a large-screen TV to air the telethon throughout the party. Not wanting to leave the building with the cash donated throughout the day, he would sleep at the community center. From sofa cushions on the floor, he'd watch the telethon and doze. Prior to leaving New Jersey, after much deliberation and debate, I decided to stay at the community center overnight and somehow finagle a kiss from Jay before daylight.

In the course of our conversations throughout my divorce, Jay confided that he was in an unhappy, unhealthy relationship which, per intel collected from our friends who were determined to get us together, had reached its nadir. That night, with much winking, nudging, and crossed fingers wagging in my face outside of Jay's field of vision, our friends left the center, and I told Jay I would stay with him. Of course, he insisted I go back to the hotel, to which I replied I couldn't see any reason for him to be alone. I'd help him guard the money.

With everyone gone and me on sofa cushions next to Jay on the floor, a quiet settled on us, and my only thought was, *How the hell am I going to pull this off?* Noticing the tiniest bit of daylight breaking, I realized the window was closing. I had to start speaking, which would put me past the point of no return. "Jay, I have a question for you." That was it. I'd jumped the shark.

From there I blabbered like an idiot, talking really fast, nearly incoherent. In the longest run-on sentence ever uttered, I said, "Jay, I'm really attracted to you, and I don't know if you know that, and I have no idea if you're attracted to me or even interested in me in any way and please understand I know you're in a relationship, and I have no interest in breaking that up I would never do that and I, of course, was just divorced and I'm not ready for a relationship but still I really am attracted to you and it's been quite some time since I've had a really good kiss so if you might be interested I'm wondering if you'd like to kiss me no pressure and if you don't want to no worries but I just wanted to ask."

To this day I cannot describe the expression on Jay's face. He did not say a single word but got up and paced around the community center. He basically walked in circles. *Lots* of them. And I could smell his brain smoking. After what seemed an eternity, he came back to the cushions, laid down and kissed me.

It was a many splendored thing and utterly surprising. In the course of a kiss, I came home—to comfort, safety, familiarity, and the deepest sense that I was exactly where I was supposed to be with exactly the person I was supposed to be with.

People started to return to the community center for the continental breakfast Jay always put out. Prior to anyone's arrival, I'd gone out into the most glorious morning I had ever seen. Crystal clear and crisp under a spectacular blue sky. The very air was vibrating. I certainly expected to enjoy kissing Jay, but I never expected this.

I had fallen in love with the man I was meant to fall in love with.

Of course, in making the decision to kiss me, Jay began to extricate himself from a great deal of sadness and sorrow. He had shared with me months earlier, when Karen made it clear he would have to choose between her and his beloved sister, Ellen, whom Karen disliked intensely, that he knew he had to end it, but just couldn't figure out how. And I needed to figure out how I would deal with seeing Karen when she arrived later that morning.

After the event, I was at Ellen's with Jay and his mom, Izzy, who never ever approved of a single girl or woman Jay dated—and there had been quite a few. Before I arrived, and mind you, not a living soul knew we had kissed, let alone fallen in love, Izzy asked him why he couldn't find someone like "that Jodi Mitchel girl." We would soon grant her wish and let her know Jay finally found someone exactly like that Jodi Mitchel girl, and was going to marry her.

CHAPTER 20
THE BUDDING AND FINAL ROMANCE

A long-distance relationship ensued. My freelance voiceover career and flexible work schedule enabled me to go to Boston on the weeks that Charlie was with his dad, and Jay came to Princeton on those weekends with some regularity. We were deliriously happy.

Having long ago broken things off with Karen, Jay and I settled into a week-on, week-off relationship with lengthy phone conversations and love letters filling the void when we could not be together.

As challenging as it was to spend a year with such distance between us, half spent *in absentia*, our relationship grew deeper with each passing week. For Jay to have come out of a difficult four-year relationship, and me through two troubled marriages, the love, trust, and comfort we found in one another made it that much sweeter and more meaningful. And at thirty-nine, the appreciation we felt for our good fortune was considerable. I spent my days exploring South Boston, reading, cooking, and finding a sense of balance, feeling emotionally secure, possibly for the first time in my life.

As our love for and commitment to one another grew, and I was beginning to feel certain that Jay was the man I wanted to spend the rest of my life with, I realized I needed to administer two litmus tests. Having dipped my pinky toe in these waters on a few occasions, I was fairly confident he'd pass, but failure on either would be a dealbreaker.

I needed first to have an unwavering commitment to the remaining gaggle. At this point, I'm twelve years off schedule. More than a freaking decade behind. If Jay passed this test, I then needed a promise that non-Jewish Jay would agree and be genuinely and perfectly comfortable raising our gaggle in the Jewish faith. All in, too. Observance of the Sabbath and holidays; religious school; bar/bat mitzvahs; confirmation from Hebrew school; the whole megillah.

This was addressed in my divorce agreement with Dean—also not Jewish—and it was profoundly important to me to raise all my children as Jews. Jay filled me with complete confidence that he could and would most happily bring up Jewish kids. Our stories were now inextricably interwoven, with our feet firmly planted on our mutual path.

With the two issues that could have brought it all crashing down now settled, life became tranquil and exhilarating—all at once. While the gaggle was still short a chick or two, the feeling that—at the age of forty, for the first time—my planets had finally aligned was glorious.

Summoning the fortitude and grit to traverse the mine-strewn landscape of my childhood often seemed impossible, but I came through it with all appendages attached. Much of my work in therapy was about understanding the trauma I suffered as a child and teenager, examining the abuse, and comprehending its effects.

Christine helped me understand that I could, as an adult, heal my inner child, whom I came to call Little Jodi. I learned that when pain is not addressed at the time of infliction or soon thereafter, the ripples don't simply dissipate. Reverberations continue until the source is addressed and understood, which can happen at any age. Christine taught me how to love, nurture, and heal Little Jodi to put an end to the cascading effects and their continued manifestation in my life as an adult, or at least lessen their effects.

It was in service to this evolving endeavor that an epiphany the size of Pluto slammed into my brain disguised as a daydream.

Working from home one afternoon, sitting at my desk, my recurring nightmare, thankfully absent for some time, played in high-definition technicolor before my wide-open eyes. There was six-year-old Little Jodi blissfully holding hands with her dad as they walked up that gorgeous green hill on a magnificent day. Stopping at the crest, my dad jumped down onto the infinite mangle of rusted metal, admonishing Little Jodi with greater and greater anger to follow. She couldn't move a muscle.

And then came me as an adult, Big Jodi, hustling up the hill. Little Jodi must've felt her coming. She turned, and that skinny little girl in torn jeans and dirty T-shirt with the crazy hair ran like hell down the hill and leapt into my arms. Wrapping her legs around my waist and arms around my neck, her face buried in my hair, I held her tighter than I'd ever held anyone or anything. You couldn't have fit a piece of paper between us.

Holding her head in my hands, our noses pressed against one another's, I told her I was there and would always be there, no matter what. She did nothing to deserve any of this, and it was not her fault. She wept in my arms as I assured her she was wonderful and adorable and incredibly strong and brave and worthy and perfectly deserving of love.

Now, almost forty, Fightin' Little Jodi stood at the crest of that hill holding Jay's loving and life-affirming hand. The infinite abyss of my nightmare gave way to my humble and heavenly dreamscape, offering promise and possibility.

From our first year together, we were able to steadily build and nurture Charlie's relationship with Jay. The top priority was to create a stable, loving, trusting, and dependable relationship between them. Charlie had been through quite enough upheaval in his short life, thank you very much, and we were wholly dedicated to providing him with emotional normalcy and security. Even though my divorce was final well before Jay and I started to date, it was appropriate and best for Charlie that our relationship progressed slowly.

At the next Labor Day fundraiser, Jay proposed on the exact spot where a year earlier I had wrangled that fateful kiss. We were positively giddy, as was everyone at the event, including Izzy, knowing that Jay had finally found his Jodi Mitchel girl. Our friends and family were over-the-moon happy for us, further warming the joy in which we were basking. Jay would move to Princeton on Halloween.

Charlie had just turned five when I sat him down on the curb on a late-September day as we walked home from school. Jay would be arriving in a few weeks, and it was time to tell Charlie. I simply said that Jay and I loved each other very much, and soon he'd move in with us, and we would be married.

In response, Charlie asked the only question to which a five-year-old who'd been through so much would need an answer. "Will Jay stay forever?" I said he would, indeed. Charlie jumped up and did the happiest happy dance ever danced. He once described Jay as the funniest man on the planet. Loving few things in life as much as laughter, Charlie was very cool with Jay's imminent arrival and permanent place in our family constellation.

At the end of October, Jay headed to Princeton, and we easily settled into cohabitation. Living without Charlie for an entire week twice a month was nearly impossible. I'll never know how I managed it. It was doubly difficult since we'd chosen not to call when he was with Dean. We didn't want Charlie to hear our voices in the middle of his time with his dad, perhaps causing him to miss us more than he might, or to disrupt their time together.

The only silver lining was that Charlie's residential schedule provided much-needed time for Jay and me to find our cadence as a couple, syncing our rhythms and heartbeats. There was a lyrical quality to this time as we built the life of our little family and planned our wedding. We were married in April at a beautiful seaside tavern and reception hall surrounded by loving, joyful family and friends. Two months later, I turned forty and started infertility treatment.

CHAPTER 21
NEARLY MIDDLE-AGED AND NOT EXACTLY OOZING FERTILITY

What followed over the next two years of trying to become pregnant were two devastating miscarriages. Some months after the last lost pregnancy, we began treatment at a clinic about an hour from home.

The first option to pursue was intrauterine insemination, or IUI, which would ultimately be administered over a period of about six months. After four fruitless inseminations with Jay's sperm came the miracle. While halting treatment to allow my body time to rest and regroup before embarking upon the next treatment option, I became pregnant "naturally."

To say we were elated would be the understatement of the epoch. Our euphoria was soon met with an equal measure of heartbreak. It seemed that from out of nowhere, I was in excruciating pain. Blood tests, pelvic exams, and ultrasounds revealed an ectopic pregnancy. The embryo had not implanted in my uterus, where it belonged, but in my fallopian tube, where it sure as hell was not supposed to be. Laparoscopic surgery was necessary to remove it—more fun.

After some weeks recovering from the surgery, we were ready for the next procedure, which was in vitro fertilization, or IVF. The meticulously timed process involved at-home stimulation of my egg production with hormone and medication injections; multiple trips to the clinic for the harvesting of said eggs and a collection of Jay's semen; injecting single sperm into a number of eggs in the lab, resulting in the development of zygotes, and monitoring their maturity into embryos; choosing embryos of the highest quality and grading, at just the right stage of development; and their implantation into my hormonally prepared uterus. Simple.

The preparation process for embryo implantation involved injections of cold progesterone oil through a syringe the thickness of my freaking pinky. Jay, like so many of his brethren, has always had a troubled relationship with needles, and as much as he wanted to support me through the injections, he was incapable of administering them. No worries. I am the least queasy person I know and had no problem injecting myself.

The first one, however, didn't go so well. After a struggle, I finally succeeded in getting the cap off the syringe. Unfortunately, the recoil caused the two-inch needle to plunge into and come out the other side of *my thumb*. That was surprising. And painful. But it sure as hell didn't stop me.

Now that my uterus was as hospitable as the goddamn Olive Garden, the supermodels of embryos would hopefully settle comfortably into their seats at the uterine table for the next nine months.

Before the first procedure, the doctor approached prior to my going under twilight sedation. As he arrived gurney-side, I said, "Doc, do me a favor. Knock me out, then knock me up." Much to my disappointment, he displayed no gurney-side manner, *whatsofuckingever*. He didn't even crack a smile. I was hurt. It was one of my better lines. Three successive IVF cycles failed.

Each failure was accompanied by indescribable and profound disappointment. Impossible to avoid was the feeling that I was a failure as a woman, and to put a finer point on it, a dried up, useless old failure of a woman. One of the most confounding elements of that emotional response, which shook me to my very foundation, was that I had been, and still am, an ardent feminist, seeing my worth and value as a woman not only in my ability to procreate, but in myriad other powers, strengths, capabilities, and talents. This failure felt nearly existential, and threw me much farther than I could have possibly known it would.

From the beginning, it seemed prudent to double-track our efforts and simultaneously pursue a pregnancy and adoption. Right smack in the middle of our dogged perseverance came a call from Journeys of the Heart adoption agency in Oregon. We chose to work with Journeys after exhaustive research, and had put together some killer marketing collateral illus-trating what a cool couple we were and how awesome Charlie was. The message was that any person finding themselves inconveniently pregnant would, of course, realize they'd be nuts not to consider us the best possible option for placement of their baby. It sure seemed unseemly, but that was the way it was done. And that was the way it was done, because that's what worked.

Andrea had just turned seventeen—just. She was a child. A child who was about to have a child. A child who, three years earlier, had been dragged out of her bed into an alley in the middle of the night, brutally raped, beaten, and left for dead. As far as we knew, she never received therapy to process this unspeakable trauma. With inexplicable strength, and despite her unstable mother's pleading that she not go through with it, Andrea engaged with Journeys to make an adoption plan.

Intermittently homeless and summoning remarkable courage, she realized she couldn't possibly raise a child. Now, a week past her due date, she asked Susan, the Director of Journeys, to reach out to us. Andrea was scheduled to be induced, enabling us to make travel arrangements and be at the hospital on the day of the birth.

Just as nine-year-old Charlie and we got into our rental car in Portland, utterly ecstatic, and headed to the hospital two hours after baby Monica, as Andrea had named her, had been pushed into the world, came the call from Susan instructing us to go to the hotel instead of the hospital. In that instant, we knew, but neither Jay nor I uttered a word. We couldn't look at one another, knowing that if we met the other's eyes, the dam would break, and a flood of devastation would drown us all.

Charlie was elated about the addition of a baby to our family. Checking the car seat at the airport in New Jersey, the agent asked if we were trav-eling with a baby. Charlie chirped, "We're on our way to pick up my baby sister!" An enormous smile spread across the agent's face, and she wished us luck. We would not obliterate Charle's joy unless we had to.

At our hotel, where Charlie occupied himself on the second bed with a book he'd brought to pass the time on our flight, with shattered hearts struggling to beat, we barely heard Susan on the phone explain that Andrea had changed her mind and would raise the baby. There was nothing to say or do and nothing to feel but anguish.

In a feeble attempt to mitigate the pain we were all reeling from, we decided to remain in Oregon for the originally intended period of time and do some sightseeing. We just couldn't bear the thought of turning on our heels and returning home without offering Charlie something positive from this trip.

Back at the airport, we checked the car seat to New Jersey and again came the question from a different agent. "Are you traveling with a baby?"

Sweet Charlie revealed his great resilience and optimism when he said, "Not this trip."

Six weeks after returning from Oregon with our empty car seat and broken hearts, Susan called one night at 11 o'clock to ask if we were still interested in adopting Andrea's baby.

Bleary-eyed and exhausted from our long work day and late evening, we emphatically told Susan we'd be on the next plane.

Andrea had been living in a motel somewhere with Monica. I can only imagine the dimension of her despondency when, now acutely aware of what motherhood entailed, she knew this was truly an impossible undertaking. I can only surmise the depth of her feelings—of failure, inadequacy, heartsickness, and perhaps even self-loathing—as she picked up the phone to ask Susan to call us.

In fact, I cannot imagine.

There was a flight out the next morning and just as we were about to leave for the airport, Susan called again, this time to inform us that she could not locate Andrea and had no idea where she was or how to reach her. The dizzying pattern that was unfolding— elation/devastation/euphoria/desperation/gigantic joy/unutterable sadness—was this close to unmanageable, threatening to separate us from our sanity at every moment.

We said we were coming and would let her know when we were on our way to Journeys.

All we could do was trust in the cosmos that Andrea would be there with the baby we intended to call Chloe. I fervently beseeched the universe to finally let us embrace this child, enfolding her in our arms and into our life. And should we be so fortunate, I also hoped that she couldn't yet hold her head up. *Ohpleaseohpleaseohplease, let her be floppy.*

CHAPTER 22
THE BUNNY

Susan was visibly relieved to tell us when we arrived that Andrea was there with the baby. After years of the gargantuan effort to bring another child into our family, I sat in breathless anticipation for Andrea to walk in the room with our daughter. A beautiful young woman appeared, holding the most exquisite baby on Earth. My reaction was the clashing antithesis of what I expected.

Thousands of harpies screeched in my head, maniacally imploring me to get out. "Are you out of your freaking mind? What the hell are you thinking?? There is no more unnatural way to have a baby!! This is a mistake! This is a huge mistake! Get out! Get out!! Get the fuck *ooooouuu-uut!*" I was paralyzed. Literally paralyzed. I could barely breathe or see or hear.

And the harpies screamed. At some point, Susan asked if I wanted to hold the baby. Of course, I said, not knowing if I was speaking in tongues. Apparently I was intelligible because Andrea walked over and placed sleeping Chloe in my arms. She was serenity personified as I hurtled toward a total emotional breakdown.

After a few minutes, Jay seemed to float toward me and took Chloe out of my arms. He held her against his chest, and she spit up down his back. He said, "Well. It's official. I'm her dad." Hearing those words out of the corner of my ear, I was extracted from the nightmare and returned, barely breathing, to the living room of Journeys of the Heart. Slowly, I regained my faculties and was able to speak.

I heard myself telling Andrea that from this moment forward Chloe would hear her story, and know who brought her into this world. We'd send pictures and stories and read Andrea's letters to her and never, never let Chloe forget where she came from. I thanked her in the most inadequate words I ever spoke for the immense gift she had bestowed upon us, and expressed how deep was our hope that she would be well and have a good life.

The car seat finally held its rightful occupant, and Jay and I shared our sadness that Charlie was not with us at this moment as he so wanted to be. Making our way through the exhilaratingly mundane moments of shopping for formula and diapers and wipes and Desitin and blankets and bonnets and bottles and choosing a darling white stuffed bunny with a pink satin bow for Chloe, then hearing a stranger remark how beautiful our baby was, all helped me begin to know and feel in every crevice of my soul that this was my child and I was her mother and all was right with the world. From that shopping spree forward, we called Chloe "Bunny." Her first tattoo two decades later was a little line drawing of a baby rabbit!

Jay, Charlie, and I experienced the indescribable happiness of bringing Chloe into our world. Good friends offered their pool to serve as a mikveh, where, with the help of our wonderful rabbi, a ritual submersion converted Chloe to Judaism. He then so generously agreed to have Chloe's naming ceremony at our temple on Rosh Hashanah, during the High Holy Days, to bestow her Hebrew name in honor of Jay's and my mother.

After three years of marriage, I decided to take my husband's name. Never intending to abandon my family surname, I took neither of my previous husband's last names and didn't expect to take Jay's. But now, having two children with different last names, neither of which was mine, it seemed prudent to become a Tolman. As Chloe received her Hebrew name, it felt fitting to change mine.

Life was idyllic, until the next unforeseen catastrophe arrived, and this one was a punch-you-in-the-gut--make-your-head-spin-at-warp-speed freaking doozy. Soon after Chloe's naming came a call from our attorney in Oregon. Andrea wanted to revoke her consent to the adoption. Jay was out of the house when the call came in. He was usually out of the house when bad news was delivered. Upon his return, I inexplicably managed to conjure my capacity for speech and told him about the call.

We soon learned that as Andrea was indigent, an attorney was assigned to her case. Since she had some quotient of Native American blood, Andrea would be represented by Oregon's leading legal expert in Native American affairs. He would invoke the Indian Child Welfare Act, a critically important law enacted in 1972 to stop the heinous practice of Indigenous children being forcibly removed from their parents and placed with white families.

Nearly a year from the day that Chloe became ours, we would return to Oregon for a three-day hearing in which expert testimony from a psychologist would be presented to speak to the bond or lack thereof forged in the time Chloe had been in our custody. A determination would then be made as to what was in her best interests.

Andrea's father was one-quarter Diné. If her attorney could find proof of his enrollment in the Navajo Nation, the case would fall under tribal jurisdiction, and we would immediately lose our daughter. She would be physically removed from us on the spot and placed in Andrea's custody. We were terrified.

The prospect of losing Chloe was beyond description. In my wildest imaginings, I could not fathom how we'd get through it. Yet, we agreed if we could somehow be assured that Andrea was able to keep Chloe healthy and safe, her rightful place would be with her birth mother. Though we felt certain that Andrea could not provide safety and stability for Chloe, we had to be sure.

Taking a chance, we reached out to the social worker with whom we knew Andrea had spoken during the adoption process to see if she could shed some light. We asked if she could legally share any information that could be helpful.

With surprising candor, the social worker expressed her absolute certainty that if Chloe were returned to Andrea, it would simply be a matter of time before she would be removed from her and placed in the foster system. She had no doubt that Andrea was incapable of caring for herself, let alone a baby, adding that she would be willing to testify to that in court.

We had our answer.

We would travel to and spend considerable time in Oregon with Chloe, meeting with a court-appointed social worker. And then, on our fourth wedding anniversary, in the eleventh hour, the day before the hearing was to begin, the decision came down. Since Andrea's lawyer was unable to find affiliation for her father with any federally-recognized tribe, Chloe would remain in our custody. The case was closed. The nightmare was over. Our daughter was ours and we were hers.

Required to appear before the judge the next morning so he could be certain Andrea understood the outcome of her case, we reiterated our promise. We would never let Chloe forget Andrea or her origins. We committed to frequent contact and assured her we most sincerely and deeply hoped she would stay in touch.

Letters and pictures and drawings and videos and stories were exchanged over the next three years. And then... nothing. Andrea fell off the map. Jay and I promised one another that as Chloe grew, we would periodically check to see if she wanted to connect with Andrea, and if she did, we would move mountains to make it happen. She expressed no interest.

Then, about four years ago, we learned that Chloe, at twenty-four years of age, had located her birth family, including Andrea, through social media. Andrea's life continued to be tragic, and for now, Chloe has chosen not to have contact with her. She does communicate with other members of her birth family, and is hoping to meet at least one of them someday soon. As for us, we remain indescribably grateful. Chloe is our cherished and beloved daughter, and our life by any measure would be profoundly diminished without her in it.

With the thankfully triumphant resolution of Chloe's case, we joyously logged her arrival in the appropriate second column. One genetic—check. One adopted—check. I was one kid closer to the gaggle, albeit seventeen years behind schedule.

CHAPTER 23
JACK THE RIPPUH!

W hen I told my mother I was pregnant at the age of forty-five, she said, "Honey, you're either very courageous or really stupid." I could've tried to defend the stupid, but I didn't have a leg to stand on.

After exhaling and finally trusting Chloe was ours, believing there was no invisible shoe threatening to kick us in the teeth, Jay and I turned our attention to the final pursuit of a pregnancy. After six years and tens of thousands of dollars spent, we resigned ourselves to the reality that we had the financial and emotional wherewithal for one last shot at it. While Jay's boys were good-looking, athletic, and perfectly viable—my girls were old, tired, and totally useless. So the donor egg route became the most pragmatic and promising.

Judy, our wonderful social worker, with whom we are in touch to this day, helped us find Laura—on paper, that is—who would become our egg donor. She was fair-complected like me, had sparkling blue eyes like Jay, dark hair like me, a theater background like both of us, a seemingly unproblematic personal and family medical history, and a good educational background. And she was young with presumably gorgeous, vital, healthy eggs.

After syncing up our cycles with more injections (and no skewered thumbs), and with Laura's girls retrieved and introduced in the lab to Jay's boys (they seemed to hit it off!), it was time for yet another implantation. We actually had photos of the embryos at various stages as the cells split multiple times. It was fascinating to see that process actually happening, not to mention life at the cellular level.

We chose to have two embryos implanted and for about three minutes hoped to have twins. Reason thankfully returned, and we implored the goddess of fertility to give us just one. Knowing in her ancient and infinite wisdom that the last thing in this world we needed was twins, she bestowed upon us a singleton.

I felt, as I did with Charlie, like Hercules. Tremendous power and energy. Invincible. Which was good, because I would need to draw on all of that when, in my sixth month, Jack turned up inverted, as in upside-down, and what is called an external inversion was necessary.

In the hospital, two obstetric nurses, standing on either side of me as I lay on yet another gurney, manipulated Jack through my belly and moved him into the proper position. And the pregnancy continued to be fabulous.

I thought I was Wonder Woman, like in not just powerful but freaking gorgeous, until Jackie Gleason entered my body in the ninth month. (You young'uns will have to look him up. It'll be worth it.) The gorgeous part at that point became, and was probably always, questionable. I really looked like Gleason with my very dark short hair and, as I had lost weight while pregnant, skinny legs and gi-*gan*-tic belly. Resembling Gleason is not something many women aspire to, but I like to think I pulled it off!

At that point, I was ready. Really, really, really ready. Unfortunately, Jack was not. At my checkup a week past due, we were told I had been leaking amniotic fluid and needed to be immediately admitted to the hospital and induced. As I had to be induced with Charlie, I knew the fun I was in for.

At the time of Jack's inversion, one of the nurses told me with some solemnity that the procedure would hurt and I shouldn't be shy about crying out or needing to squeeze a nurse's hand. That gave me pause. Giant, hairy pause.

The inversion was practically painless. The nurses kept asking if I was okay and seemed shocked that I was feeling so little discomfort. This made me feel indestructible and quite hopeful about my capacity to manage the pain of labor this time. I was wrong—terrible, horribly, woefully, regretfully wrong.

Induction is not fun. When contractions increase in intensity and frequency with a slow and gradual build-up, as they do in the natural progression of labor, a pregnant person knows what to expect with the coming contraction and can prepare mentally and physically for the pain. Induction causes contractions to start at the top of the chart with no gradual buildup or opportunity to prepare.

Ouch is a wee bit of an understatement. *"ARE YOU FREAKING KIDDING ME???"* is a fucking understatement!

As I felt eleven years ago with Charlie, I was certain my bones were breaking. It's at this point it becomes clear that the body capable of withstanding labor and birth is not human, but a cyborg or bionic or a superhero or alien or magic or something otherworldly. It simply seems impossible for the human body to undergo this torture and live to tell the tale, let alone come back and do it again!!

But endure we must, and endure we do. Inexplicably.

After many hours of unproductive labor, I was told it was time to push.

Wait. What? Push? Push?? Did someone say push?? Who the hell thinks I have the strength to push, for Chrissakes?? I'm forty-six freaking years old!! I may as well be a hundred and forty-six!

With Charlie, my body made it clear it was not wild about giving up its babies. I hold onto many things, often well past the point of reason—grudges, fat, hope. And so it was with Jack. Like Charlie, Jack had gone seven days past due. Getting my hair cut well after he was supposed to have arrived, the stylist asked when I was due. I said, "A week ago."

She said, "I'll hurry."

I pushed my brains out with Charlie and broke every blood vessel in my eyes. Lookin' lovely, as usual. I did the same with Jack, but things were not progressing, so an emergency C-section was in order.

Being wheeled into the OR, I asked the attending surgeon to please set up a mirror so I could watch the surgery and delivery. He said, "No."

With my temperature spiking and fury rising, I said, "What do you mean, no?? This is *my* baby!"

He said, "Right. And this is *my* OR."

Goddammit!!!!

Jay is a lifetime member-in-good-standing of the Squeamish Squad. I have no clue how he did it but he remained heroically vertical throughout the entire experience. He looked only into my eyes and impressively did not pass out while cutting the umbilical cord.

When my OB lifted Jack out of my belly, I was able to pick my head up and get a glimpse of him, slightly terrified to see he looked like an eggplant. I felt confident in my recollection that our egg donor was white, so I was a bit confused about where this color came from. Then the OB nurses took Jack, worked their magic, and he soon "pinked" up.

When they finally placed him on my chest, my OB shared with us the reason Jack did not advance down the birth canal, and a C-section was necessary. He was face-up. In that position, a baby's head cannot move into the canal. When she opened me, she was surprised to see Jack's eyes wide open, staring right at her. Leave it to Jack.

Happily, I was able to stay in the hospital for a few days, which was sheer heaven. I'd nurse Jack, love him up, and they'd take him away. It was quiet!! I could sleep!! *Sleep*, I tell you!!

Jack was born exactly two years to the day that Chloe's adoption was finalized. An auspicious day in our family. Jay's dad would come up from Florida for the month of August every year, and return home after our Labor Day fundraiser. Having him in New Jersey when Jack was born was particularly delicious.

As Jay, his dad, and I were leaving the hospital with Jack to take him home, an elderly gentleman with an uncanny resemblance to the old prospectors from those iconic Westerns was on his way in. We were sure he'd busted into the moonshine on the wagon ride over. Hearing John loudly fawning over the baby on our way to the car, Grizzly called out in a loud, growly, and surprisingly theatrical voice, "Jack the Rippuh!!" It stuck. A "rippuh" he was and a "rippuh" he remains.

Compared to the great difficulty that befell Charlie as a little boy in the wake of his father's and my divorce, and the uncertainty and upheaval that accompanied the first nine months of Chloe's life, Jack sailed into this world unencumbered. He was born into a happy, functional family with a brother and sister who could not have loved him more. And his parents—who, after moving heaven and Earth—were ecstatically happy, fulfilled, and finally at peace.

And thus, in the year of our Lord, 1998, eighteen years after The Decision was made on that fateful bed, in that consequential apartment, on that pivotal day, the third and final column had its entry. One genetic—

check! One adopted—check! One from a donor egg—check! The gaggle was complete—not huge, but blissfully complete.

I was forty-six and felt ninety-six, but I had to bounce back to twenty-six. I had no choice. When I told Jay a year later that I'd love to adopt another baby, he said, "You'll have to do that with another husband."

I said, "Don't tempt me.

Here's a wonderful aside for you and a bit of a flashforward. Jack and Haley, his fabulous "sigo," started to go out a few years ago. On their first in-person date, Haley asked Jack a fascinating question. She wanted to know something about him that very few people, if any, knew. He shared that he was a donor egg baby. Haley was blown completely away and shared that she was a donor sperm baby. I mean, really, what are the flipping odds?!

Quite a few years ago, Haley completed genetic testing through 23and-Me. She matched with her paternal grandfather and was able to connect with him. With his son's permission, he shared her donor's email address, and Haley reached out. Her donor-dad, as she affectionately refers to him, was open to meeting, and they have created a close and loving relationship. He went on to have two children with his partner, and they—Haley, Haley's mom, and Jack—periodically get together. Very cool.

CHAPTER 24
BACK FROM THE BRINK

Copious research over many decades tells us that abused children often grow up to become abusive parents. I believe that without some sort of intervention, be it from a concerned family member or friend, or therapy, or a conscious and deliberate engagement in self-reflection, with a commitment to learn, develop, and practice loving and healthy parenting skills, the victim of abuse can easily fall into that horrible trap. It sure seemed like I was headed in that direction.

Observing Jay's approach to parenting, especially when juxtaposed with my own, enlightened and empowered me to step back from the trigger of that trap. Thanks to a congenital patience deficiency, especially when stressed, not to mention the amount of rage I ingested throughout my upbringing, I developed a propensity for yelling at the kids, pressuring them to hurry up and finish that and come here and go there and tell me this and take care of that. In my worst moments, I could feel my fury rushing to the surface, fast approaching the endpoint of my control. It felt like one day, any minute...

Somehow, something—I honestly don't know what—interceded. Perhaps it was simply my awareness and fear of what I felt coming. There was a governor in me that stopped me in my tracks. I would go so far and no farther. But it so often felt like it was just a matter of time.

Maybe I was wrong. Maybe I would never have crossed that line.

Perhaps I would have managed to maintain control and not fall into the deep end. But, it felt possible. And the mere possibility struck great fear in me.

Jay's seemingly unflappable nature, coupled with invaluable coping strategies, control mechanisms, and methods of clearly seeing the real priorities, equipped him with what seemed to me to be nearly bottomless patience. He parented with an even hand. He was reasonable, appropriate, calm, and soft-spoken. In comparison, it became clear I was on a trajectory heading to a destination where, if reached, I could not live with myself.

The fallout of fear and shame settled on me after causing Chloe to burst into tears over some stupid and immediate need I had for her to do something other than what she was doing at that moment. That was my tipping point. It felt like those near-death visions when a person's entire life flashes before their eyes, spanning every single moment of experience since birth in a nanosecond.

And in that nanosecond, a stark image was imprinted of my woefully insufficient capacity for patience and control. I count it as the greatest accomplishment of my life that I was able to realize and understand what might lay ahead and choose a different path. And I fully credit my husband who, by demonstrating every day what patient, calm parenting looked and sounded like, showed me how to be a mom to my children while standing well back from the brink.

CHAPTER 25
CHARLIE

Charlie was a breeze. It often happens that new parents struggle with a million worries and anxieties. That didn't happen with Charlie. Not because of anything I did or didn't do, was or wasn't, but because of Charlie. He was downright tranquil. Parenting him was a walk on the most beautiful beach on a splendiferous day. That is until that crazy bout of postpartum hit, and then, not so much. But he seemed unfazed by it. He remained even-tempered, calm, and seemingly imperturbable. From the moment I laid eyes on him, smelled him, touched him, heard him... I walked on air.

There may be certain joys one can imagine without the benefit of experience. There are others that are unknowable until the universe bestows the greatest gift beyond imagination. When the magnificence and magnitude of the love one feels for one's child is experienced, it defies all expectation, comprehension, and capacity. Miraculous is the most accurate descriptor.

Even pedestrian tasks take on the tenor of the extraordinary, and one moves through them in a state of bliss. And abject exhaustion. The depths of the fatigue are also unknowable until you are that deeply, incomprehensibly, bone-crushingly wiped out. But you wouldn't change it for anything on Earth.

Soon after Charlie was born, my Aunt Ruth called to congratulate me and asked how I was feeling. I said, "Incredibly happy and so tired." She told me to prepare to feel tired for the next twenty years. Also guilty. Spoken like one Jewish mother to another.

When Charlie was a newborn, my mother was convinced there was something seriously wrong with his head. It was too large. Since Google didn't yet exist, I couldn't search the normal circumference of a newborn's head. Periodically throughout her visits, she actually took to measuring his noggin with a tape measure. I assured her the size of his head was due to the massive brain he inherited from his mother. Somehow, even as a new parent, I was not a bit worried. His head looked pretty freaking normal to me.

Thankfully, as time passed, so did my mother's obsession with Charlie's cranium. One of my obsessions, however, plagued me until Charlie was eighteen months old.

At the time of his birth, routine circumcision was a controversial issue. A vocal movement asserted that circumcision was unnecessary and subjected a child to avoidable trauma. As Charlie's father and I wrestled with the decision, we asked the pediatrician for his opinion. He said it was not necessary for hygiene or genital health, as long as a boy was taught how to properly care for himself. Seemed reasonable.

However, as a Jewish mother, I was deeply conflicted. Had we decided to go forward with circumcision, it would have had to be done eight days after his birth by a mohel, a person who performs ritual Jewish circumcision. His non-Jewish father and I agreed at the last possible minute not to circumcise Charlie. And every time I changed his diaper or bathed him, I could barely stand it.

An opportunity presented itself when Charlie was eighteen months old. He had been born with undescended testicles. I know that doesn't sound like much of an opportunity, but stick with me here.

The pediatrician assured us this was not at all unusual, and it often happens that the testes descend in due time. He did say, however, that if they did not appear on their own and move into their apartment by the time Charlie was eighteen months old, surgery to retrieve them would be necessary. Since Charlie's studio remained vacant by the time he hit the eighteen-month mark, we knew that surgery was imminent.

I asked the doctor if Charlie could be circumcised at the time of the surgery. I had not told him when Charlie was born that we were Jewish, but as I grappled with my dilemma, I shared it with him. He was a devout Catholic and a true believer in strict adherence to religious practices and rituals. In that context, he expressed his opinion that Charlie should absolutely be circumcised, and there would be no issue in doing it at the time of the procedure.

Seeking additional guidance, I reached out to the rabbi in the synagogue where I grew up, asking where on the spectrum of ritual importance circumcision fell. He solved my quandary by saying the two most important traditions in all of Judaism, and there are *many*, are observance of the Sabbath and circumcision, a sign of the covenant between God and the Jewish people.

So there it was. I mean, who the hell was I to break the freaking covenant?? Fortunately, Charlie's dad agreed to have Charlie circumcised.

The rabbi had informed me that in order for the circumcision to be ritualistically valid, a mohel would need to be present in the OR. Not belonging to a synagogue at the time, nor engaged with the local Jewish community, I couldn't easily find a mohel, let alone one willing to be in an operating room in Philadelphia while a doctor performed a circumcision. I managed to find a mohel who happened to be a hundred and thirty-six years old, with a one hundred and seventeen-year-old driver who brought him to the hospital and helped him make his way to the OR. The pediatrician assisted him in preparing to enter and welcomed him into his operating room.

Dean and I were with Charlie, of course, as he was prepared for surgery. He was removed from my arms by a nurse, who carried him down the hall and out of sight. Although it was routine surgery, that was the most terrifying moment of my life. Losing sight of Charlie as the nurse rounded a corner, I was consumed with one horrific thought. I may never see him again. Alive, that is. As we all know, shit happens. And some shit is worse than other shit.

In relatively short order, my very-much-alive Charlie was returned to my arms, and I realized with tremendous relief the great boon in all of this was that he was circumcised under general anesthesia. I'm sure Jewish mothers the world over would've given their left anything if it could've happened this way for their sons.

Miraculously, Charlie was in very little discomfort following the procedure and came through it like all good little Jewish boys… nipped, tucked, and a member in good standing of the Tribe. And this Jewish mother was able to view her son in his nakedness and know that all was right as ritually-appropriate rain.

Charlie was simply the most delicious living thing I had ever seen, with gorgeous curls and an angelic smile. Simply laying my eyes upon him created an indescribable sensation of bliss. Now I knew the real reason I decided at twenty-six that no matter what it took, I'd become a mother.

And he was hysterically funny. Especially when he became old enough to experience the high induced by causing laughter in others. Just as my mom and I thought the other was the funniest person alive, that's how I feel about Charlie. No one makes me laugh harder.

We spent a vacation week on Long Beach Island in New Jersey when Charlie was six. Soon after unpacking his stuff, he came downstairs wearing every single piece of clothing we brought for him. Every sock, T-shirt, pair of shorts, hat, etc. If he could have put on multiple pairs of shoes, he would have. He looked like a very small, very colorful Michelin Man.

After a shower, Charlie loved to run around naked upstairs, air-drying. One evening, we heard a loud "Ow!!" Jay called up to make sure he was okay. Charlie responded, "I just slapped my penis for no apparent reason!" As was mandated by the federal Humiliate Your Children in Your Toast at Their Wedding Act, that little anecdote made its way into Jay's tribute to Charlie and Julie, his absolutely fabulous wife, when they got hitched. Luckily, neither objected!

Ironically, and even more hilarious than his attempts at hilarity, was Charlie's degree of seriousness under certain circumstances, such as when in costume. When Charlie was two, I dressed him as a prizefighter for Halloween in a tiny terrycloth hooded robe, the littlest boxing gloves, and a shiner drawn with an eyebrow pencil. When he was three, he was a firefighter in a huge red plastic helmet, with a fire-engine-red fire engine I made from a cardboard box, suspended from his shoulders by twine. He could barely move without banging his truck into everything within a three-foot radius of his body, but he was determined to trick or treat all night.

Purim is a Jewish holiday where kids dress in costume and parade around the synagogue as the story of the historical events is retold in the Purim spiel. In the parade, when Charlie was five and six, he was dressed as Hamen, the bad guy in the story, complete with brown pipe-cleaner Snidely Whiplash mustache. The following year, he was the good guy, King Ahasuerus, in his flowing robes and brown pipe-cleaner beard, carrying a bejeweled scepter three feet taller than Charlie. Throughout the festivities, he never cracked a smile. Not that he was unhappy. He was in a state of thrall, taking his assumed identities as seriously as Christian Bale. You didn't mess with Charlie when he was in costume.

Charlie's dad remarried when he was four—Charlie was four, his Dad was older—and soon had two kids with his new wife. Now a big brother, Charlie was thrilled to welcome his baby brother and then a sister into his dad's family. He seemed to adjust to the huge changes in his life quickly and well, but around the age of seven, the trauma of the divorce began to emerge. We knew it was there under the surface from the beginning, as Charlie bounced off the walls every transition day, but he started to show signs of increased emotional distress.

He described a nightmare he'd had about being abandoned that had clearly thrown him for a loop. He needed to know at all times which room we were in, how long we'd be in that room, which room we'd be in next, and how long we'd stay there. Jay and I became increasingly concerned and started him in therapy with a wonderful child psychologist.

Jonathan occasionally scheduled sessions for Jay and me to help us help Charlie. In one of our meetings, I broke down, weeping about the damage I feared Charlie had suffered, worrying that we were somehow causing further harm. I cried, "I'm just afraid we're going to fuck him up."

Jonathan gently and with great compassion responded, "Of course, you're going to fuck him up. It's inevitable. Every parent fucks up their kid to some degree, one way or another. And they come through it, just like we did."

Jay and I realized that all we could do was our very best to help Charlie navigate the complex maze that was his life.

Visiting my folks in Florida when Charlie was six years old, I took him to see *Huckleberry Finn* at the local movie theater. He loved the story of Huck. During a particularly dark and disturbing scene, Huck is chased around their cabin by his drunk father, wielding a rather large cleaver. Terrified, Charlie blurted out in the dark theater, "Mom! What made you think this movie was appropriate for me??" Verbatim. Amidst uproarious laughter from the audience, I rescued Charlie to the warmth and stillness of a Florida evening, where we sat on a bench, and I held him for quite a while.

A sweet memory of Charlie and his friend Zach was when they talked to the interior lights in Jay's car. Jay had the kids believing the lights were alive and could speak to them. The control for the lights was out of sight when the kids were in the backseat. Jay said the lights could answer yes or no questions, and they could ask anything they wanted.

Their queries were so loving, tender, sensitive, and hilarious. They asked if it was all right to tell their friends that the lights could talk to them. They wanted to be sure not to betray the confidence of the lights if they preferred their power be kept secret. Knowing if word got out, he would be overrun with neighborhood kids wanting to talk to the lights, Jay wisely had the lights respond with an unequivocal "No." And to our knowledge, Charlie and Zach never told a soul.

For Charlie's tenth birthday, we took him and his cousin, Alex, to Baltimore to see the Inner Harbor and an Orioles game. Walking to Camden Yards from our hotel, we encountered a homeless man sleeping on the street. Charlie had never seen such a sight and asked who the man was and why he was lying on the sidewalk. I explained he did not have a home or anywhere to sleep. I knew exactly what was coming.

With great excitement, Charlie said, "We can help him! We have an extra bedroom! He can live with us!!" Trying to offer an acceptable reason why that was not possible was one of the greatest parenting challenges I ever faced. My heart broke for my empathetic boy as he desperately tried to understand how it could be that we would not help someone in such great need, especially when it seemed we could.

And then there were the occasional screw-ups. Case in point... one evening we had company for dinner—actually, we had chicken—and were all seated around the dining room table. Chloe was three and Charlie twelve. We asked Charlie to keep an eye on his sister while they played in the family room, out of sight of all of us in the dining room. Noticing after a while that it was very quiet, Jay went to check on them.

Charlie was on the computer on the desk in the corner with his back to the room, absorbed in his favorite game, *Need for Speed*. Chloe was nowhere to be seen. A noise from inside the fireplace revealed she had climbed in, closed the screen, and was blissfully playing in the soot, as if it were her own private sandbox. Jay reached in and pulled her out, calmly saying "Charlie, I thought you were watching Chloe."

Charlie turned from the computer to see Chloe, who was covered from head to toe in thick blackness, looking like she had fallen into a vat of black paint. He was appalled as the potential calamity of his oversight dawned on him. From then on, he became the most trustworthy babysitter we could've asked for.

Charlie seemed to breeze through John Witherspoon Middle School—singing in their fabulous chorus, Witherspoon Sixteen; playing Little League baseball; honing his craft as a ballet dancer; appearing in the annual performance of *The Nutcracker*; and continuing to pursue his love of art and music—all alongside a wonderful group of kids who formed his tight and loving circle of friends.

We celebrated his bar mitzvah as he chanted a daunting Torah portion and Haftorah in our synagogue. Jay and I were thrilled to take Charlie to Israel to commemorate his bar mitzvah with a group from our temple.

He suffered his first heartbreak when a girl he liked—who'd convinced him she liked him back—broke up with him without explanation and refused to speak to him again. He was blindsided and confused, with not a shred of understanding of what just happened. My thoughts turned to trucks.

I tried to explain to Charlie that girls sometimes behave in ways that cannot be understood, especially when it comes to romance. My woefully inadequate explanation did nothing to mitigate his grief, and I could only wait for the pain to pass. Thankfully, it did, and Charlie was able to pick himself up and carry on with his young life.

High school was filled with more romance: singing in a new *a cappella* group called the Testostertones (Ha!); larger roles in *The Nutcracker* with each consecutive year; very good grades; the emergence of an eclectic and insatiable reader; wonderful friendships filled with filmmaking; inventions of skateboards equipped with parachutes made from trash bags to break their speed when careening down a steep hill; confirmation from Hebrew school; two proms to which he wore crazy creative outfits; and a broken leg from playing soccer in the rain. Charlie's misery and frustration at having a broken leg the summer before heading off to college was palpable. He colorfully expressed his lamentation. "Mom! This fucking sucks! It was supposed to be my balls-to-the-wall summer!!"

College plans were in the making. Having excellent grades and SAT scores and being a male ballet dancer, had us assuming Charlie would stand in good stead with his top college choices—Vassar, Wellesley, and Middlebury. When the third rejection letter came in and I was jumping up and down, tearing my hair out, my wise and calm child said, "Mom, I'm going to college. We just don't know where yet." It was always remarkable to me when my kids demonstrated how much more mature they were than their mother.

At that point, we decided to visit Charlie's safety schools and went back to Baltimore to see Goucher, a small liberal arts college. We were all quite impressed. Charlie seemed to love it and felt it was an excellent fit.

Dropping my firstborn off at college was much more difficult than I could've imagined, and I imagined it was something I was constitutionally incapable of doing. With the family gathered in Charlie's dorm room at the end of the day saying our goodbyes, I decided to drag him back to the car. He's 6-foot-5, but I was motivated.

His room was on the third floor, so the stairs would be a challenge. Of course, there was the elevator. As I mapped out the quickest route, Jay knew what was happening in my head. Thankfully, he helped me exit Charlie's room without humiliating myself or springing a hernia. It was weeks before I could wrap my heart around his absence. As soon as I knew he had made some friends, was having fun, enjoying classes, and doing exactly what he should be doing—becoming an independent and actualized individual—I was able to manage the milestone.

Charlie enjoyed significant recognition throughout college for several notable projects, among them a large installation on the main campus of a series of four-foot-tall steel ocean waves he forged in the studio; production of an impressive avant-garde sound sculpture exhibit; performances in several dance productions; and regularly making the dean's list. Four years went by in a flash. And my sanity held, such as it was.

Charlie's experiences in college led to a passion for lighting design, which is where he found work after graduation in theater, film, and TV in New York. Perhaps his most exciting project was lighting Beyoncé for a New Year's Eve TV special where she performed on a barge on the Hudson River, surrounded by floating platforms from which the most spectacular fireworks were launched into the night sky.

My dad was so proud of this accomplishment that he told all his neighbors and friends about Charlie working with BeeYounce. (I worked hard to get my dad to say her name as often as I possibly could.) He went on to obtain a master's in lighting design from Rensselaer Polytechnic. After completing the program, he was offered a position in their Lighting Research Center as a research scientist working on designing and creating lighting for all applications: automotive, medical, industrial, residential, commercial, etc. Throughout, Charlie produced art and ultimately decided to leave the LRC to pursue a Master of Fine Arts from the Tyler School of Art and Architecture, where he is currently studying glass blowing and casting. He's in heaven, and we're floating right beside him.

CHAPTER 26
CHLOE

C hloe was simply the most serene baby we ever saw. She rarely cried. There was no such thing as swaddling her too tightly. And she'd sleep through anything, including live, excruciatingly loud music. She would wake without a sound. Lying perfectly quiet in her bassinet next to our bed, we'd have to look to see if she was awake. She had a gorgeous moon face, huge black eyes, and a Cupid's bow mouth, always looking like she was awaiting a kiss.

My dad was legendary for finding a phrase he liked and relentlessly running it into the ground. His favorite was "Chloe's eyes are like black diamonds." I simply cannot imagine how many times we heard him say it from the day he first saw her until he left this world. And he was right.

Her first birthday after our case was settled was a huge neighborhood-wide affair in our yard. Everyone knew what had happened and that it had been successfully resolved, and we wanted to celebrate! Tons of food, an enormous cake, music, balloons, and Andre the Magic Bean, a really bad clown bordering on disturbing who I'd found online. We never figured out why he called himself a bean, let alone a magic one. He was stick-skinny, wore very little clown make-up, had a bit of a stubble, wasn't funny or particularly talented, and slightly creeped us out. Still, it was the most fabulous party I can ever remember.

Soon after her birthday, I took Chloe to school to see DooDah—as she called Charlie—when he was in the fourth grade. His teacher wanted to meet Chloe since she'd heard so much about her from Charlie and his friends, and came out into the hall with him to say hello. She commented on her huge eyes. Charlie said, "Chloe's eyes are so big, she can see the whole world." My heart melted.

Developing a unique language as she started to verbalize, Chloe called our dog Shirley "Froolah." Alligator was "ayegogog," as in "See ya later, ayegogog!" Ice cream was "icekabinga." Marbles were "mahbums."

And speaking of Shirley, Chloe was three-ish, upstairs entertaining herself one quiet afternoon when I went up to see what she was up to. Hearing me coming, she came to the top of the stairs with her arms outstretched, palms upward, covered with something thick and black. I couldn't figure out what I was looking at. She led me into our bedroom upon my asking what was on her hands, where Shirley was lying on the floor as our Golden Retriever, Mamie, was happily licking her. All over.

Shirley was quite large with wiry hair. My mother used to say she looked like she'd been shot out of a cannon. Upon closer examination, I noticed Shirley looked shiny. I asked Chloe if she had put something on her. She walked me into the bathroom, where I found a huge, nearly empty jar of Vaseline, which I knew had never been touched. I'm assuming I need not offer any further detail. I don't know how long it took Mamie to get Shirley clean nor how much fur she ingested, but after her spa treatment, Shirley was a lot softer than I'd remembered. And Mamie was regular for the remainder of her life.

Charlie and his friends couldn't get enough of Chloe. They'd take turns holding her in their laps, and she was captivated. Charlie and Zach loved to co-author stories that were riotously funny. My favorite was "Fighter Pilot Chloe," complete with illustrations inspired by baby Chloe in her carrier, looking to the boys like a fighter pilot in her cockpit. Fearless Fighter Pilot Chloe raced through the skies on her missions, shooting down bad guys with ease!

Jack came along when Chloe was two. She adored him and loved to decorate him. I came into the bedroom one afternoon to find Jack in his carrier in the middle of our bed and noticed a bunch of things on his head. Chloe had gotten into a large bag of buttons of all sizes, shapes, and colors and created button constellations on Jack's head. He was perfectly content to let her do her thing, and she had been at it for hours.

She loved to give Jay haircuts. He'd sit on the floor, and she'd work on him for as long as he'd let her. With a pair of child's scissors that couldn't cut air, she picked up locks of his hair and "cut," providing sound effects as she went. "Snap snap. Snap snap."

As I returned home from work one day, Chloe's sitter, Marlenie, reported that Chloe had been so quiet upstairs in her room for the longest time. She went up to check on her. Pushing the door open and poking her head in, Marlenie found the room filled with a gigantic cloud of something. Chloe had taken a full container of baby powder and sprinkled it on every surface. Marlenie calmly asked Chloe what she was doing when Chloe shouted, "Close the door! I'm cleaning!!" Actually, I would be the one cleaning.

With a friend from nursery school over for a play date, I could hear the girls busy downstairs in the playroom. "Chloe! You're a bossy boss!!" said Rachel.

To which my daughter replied, "I'm not bossy. I'm right."

I knew right then I'd never have to worry about this kid.

As a parent, you talk to your children and never know if they're hearing you or will remember a word you say. Chloe answered that question for me in kindergarten. When our kids argued over who got more candy, had more juice, less screen time, was being shortchanged, or cheated in some way, I would put a stop to it by insisting it didn't matter who had more or less. Life is not a contest! Chloe's kindergarten teacher shared a story about one of the kids calling out that he finished his drawing first, beating everybody. Chloe, so shy she could barely speak in front of anyone outside the family, piped up with, "Life is not a contest!" I was floored.

She had her first experience with mean girls in first grade. Her class was in line in the hall after recess. She was standing between her two besties, Christie and Julianna. They were excitedly chatting about something or other, and at some point, Chloe had something to say. With Chloe between them, Christie told Julianna not to listen to Chloe and pulled her away as she issued the directive. They ignored Chloe for the rest of the day. The fact that she shared this with me after school was a testament to the degree of her devastation.

I can count on one hand the number of times in her life I've seen Chloe cry. Telling me what Christie and Julianna did was one of those times. Even as a kid, Chloe played life very close to the vest. She was inscrutable. Knowing what she was feeling or thinking at any given moment was nearly impossible. But this hurt her so much that she had to let it out. Yet another truck scenario drove through my head.

Chloe asked me not to say or do anything, and I respected her wishes. She somehow managed to have close friendships with Christie and Julianna throughout elementary and part of middle school—another indication that she was resilient and strong. I remember feeling stunned and shattered that she experienced this "mean girls" thing so young. I was fully expecting it in middle or high school, but sure as hell not in the first grade.

What we always thought of as shyness in Chloe revealed itself to be severe social anxiety. As an introvert, she had great difficulty managing social situations. When an adult talked to Chloe, not only could she not look at them or answer... it seemed she'd attempt to crawl inside us.

She was diagnosed in fourth grade with inattentive ADHD. Several teachers had reported that while it appeared she paid no attention in class and was constantly daydreaming, when asked about the lesson at hand, she was able to repeat the teachers' lessons almost word-for-word. Her anxiety rendered her incapable of engaging with the neuropsychologist who tested her, so we never did get a definitive diagnosis, but there was no question after reading extensively about the disorder that she had ADHD. We discovered medication was not an option, but we helped her find her strategies and coping mechanisms, enabling her to be remarkably successful throughout her entire academic career.

I instilled in Chloe at an early age a righteous sense of feminism and belief in the cause of equality for girls and women. In second grade she founded the Chloe Club, with the fabulous tagline "Get the Power to be a Girl!" Jay still has his laminated membership card, honored to have been one of the only males allowed entry, along with Jack and Charlie. This was one of the earliest indications that as a devout introvert with substantial social anxiety, she had the ability to come out of herself and even be a leader when she so desired. It was gratifying and such a relief to see, as we often wondered how those characteristics would affect her.

Quite a few incidents throughout her life revealed Chloe's tenacity and fierce determination to rise to difficult occasions. Her bat mitzvah was a major accomplishment. Close friends who knew her well and empathized with her social anxiety, shared with us after the fact that they wondered how she would manage, and how she would come through such a public "performance." She wowed everyone.

Not only was she able to accomplish all the daunting tasks associated with a bat mitzvah, such as chanting in Hebrew from the Torah, leading prayers, and delivering a speech in front of the entire congregation, but she spoke from a personal vantage point in an emotionally revealing and moving speech. Clearly, Chloe had the ability to step up to any plate, regardless of how high it might be heaped with difficulty.

Interviewing at colleges was another example of her strength of will and downright doggedness. Knowing how challenging it was for her to speak to strangers, and how important a component of the application and acceptance process personal interviews were, we were quite concerned. Add to that the stress level inherent in the process, given how high the stakes were. Would she be able to traverse this landscape? It was nearly impossible to imagine she could, especially at Sarah Lawrence, a small, "fring-ey" liberal arts college in New York, which was her top choice.

We had the good fortune to run into the graduate student later in the day who had interviewed her. She was enthusiastic and expressive about her impressions of Chloe, and what a remarkable young woman she found her to be. Of course we knew all of that, but her ability to surmount her personal obstacles in such an anxiety-provoking and fraught circumstance was remarkable. Once again, she showed us, and much more importantly, herself, that she was gritty and indefatigable.

Chloe was our little hunter-gatherer/nature girl who loved to scavenge and search for things in the woods across from our house. If she found animal bones, which she did from time to time, she was thrilled. She didn't handle them until she researched online how to safely do so, then donned latex gloves, brought the fragments home, boiled them, bleached them, and added them to her gruesome collection of objects. She is currently working on a very large shadow box filled with an arrangement of the various bones and fragments collected throughout her life.

Her favorite summers were spent at the Princeton Friends Camp, a no-frills day camp where the entire day was spent outside building things, lashing things, digging in the dirt, making mud, baking with mud, sculpting with mud, painting with mud, wearing mud, eating mud, and basically staying as filthy as humanly possible all day.

Exhibiting very specific proclivities, she started devouring the *Nancy*

Drew series, one book after another, transfixed. An avid interest in crime developed, and soon, she couldn't get enough of the various TV shows related to forensics and psychological profiling of criminals. A sizable dark streak and macabre sensibilities were discovered when, at the age of seven, she wrote her first poem.

Composed on the computer, complete with a Gothic font, she printed it out and tacked it to her closet door. On my way through her room one Saturday afternoon, I found the poem and showed it to Jay, asking if he thought it was something we should be concerned about.

Entitled "The Death of Mary Lu," it read:

The death has come upon me
I feel it sucking the life out of me
I will die
When it finishes me off,
I shall die
The death has come for me
It shall come for you some day
Just as it came for me

We decided to do nothing and wait to see if she murdered anyone.

On a family outing to Barnes and Noble, after entering the store and fanning out to our respective areas of interest, Chloe, ten at the time, later found me in a far corner of the store. She sheepishly approached, clutching a large coffee table book to her chest, its cover against her body.

"Mommy, may I have this book?"

"Show me what it is, sweetheart, and I can let you know."

Hesitantly, she turned the book around with its cover now visible. In the center was a photograph of Ted Bundy, surrounded by photos of Jeffrey Dahmer, John Wayne Gacy, Albert DeSalvo, and the Zodiac Killer. I asked if she thought it would keep her up at night. With confidence, she assured me it would not. I said, "OK. But if it starts to creep you out, you can let me know, and we'll put it away for a while. Deal?"

"Deal," she said.

She read it from cover to cover, memorizing every grisly detail. She actually became quite the expert on the profiles of serial killers.

When Charlie was nearly finished with college, and Chloe and Jack were in the fifth and third grades, we made the decision to move to the South Shore of Boston where Jay grew up. We both had siblings in Massachusetts, and wanted to be near the water and expose the younger kids to sailing and skiing, both of which Charlie was already into and Jay grew up doing and truly loved. It was then that Chloe revealed her mercenary tendencies.

We were in the playroom as I filled trash bag after bag with stuff to move or give away while Chloe lazed on a loveseat, observing as I worked my ass off, not offering to lift a finger to help. I said, "How about I give you your very own trash bag so you can pack up some stuff you'd like to take?"

With impeccable timing, she said, "How about you give me my very own twenty-dollar bill? Then I'll get started."

Being a university town with all its cultural opportunities, Princeton offered a magnificently diverse community with students from all over the world in the kids' classrooms and our neighborhood. It was religiously diverse as well, with a sizable Jewish population and a vibrant Jewish Center. As a university town, Princeton boasted a fantastic public school system, rivaling any private school in the country, which is one reason property taxes were exorbitant.

An imminent reassessment of the town was about to double our taxes, soon to render Princeton pretty much unaffordable for us. Despite that reality, leaving was a tough decision to make. We knew Boston's South Shore was quite white and WASP-y. It was also difficult to leave the community in which Charlie grew up, where so many of his friends returned from college to spend time with their families.

After many months deliberating, Jay and I decided to make the move since Charlie would soon graduate college and be off to who knew where. With Chloe and Jack still so young, we wanted them to experience the lifestyle New England had to offer, as well as be physically close to our siblings. It would be a mixed bag, for sure. The tiny town of Cohasset is a gorgeous seaside hamlet with a very good public school system; the little ones proceeded to settle in nicely with seemingly little effort.

When Chloe was twelve, we discovered CSI camp, the closest on the SUNY campus in Cobleskill, New York. She attended CSI camp for two consecutive summers, each offering week-long programs where the kids investigated simulated crime scenes recreated from actual unsolved crimes.

One scene was in an apartment using a blow-up sex doll as the body, and one an actual burned-out car with a crash dummy in the trunk. Daily classes covered various elements of forensic science: preserving evidence at a scene; bagging and gathering evidence; preserving the chain of custody of evidence; analyzing DNA using their own and comparing samples; gathering and preserving prints of all kinds; analyzing fibers, blood and blood spatters and bones, hair, and clothing; etc. The kids presented their findings to the "grand jury" composed of parents and staff, after which a determination was made whether criminal charges should be brought.

In both cases, the juries made the same determinations as the actual juries made. It was impressively professional and comprehensive, and Chloe was in her element. For quite some time, she felt she wanted to become a forensic profiler for the FBI. So much so that when she was in the tenth grade, we toured the Henry C. Lee Institute of Forensic Science at the University of New Haven. Lee had become famous as the lead forensic expert on the O.J. Simpson murder trial. By the time Chloe was ready to decide which colleges she would apply to, her interests had shifted. But she never left the dark side.

Chloe, like Charlie, was academically successful throughout high school, developing an independent and out-of-the-box approach to the conventional curriculum. She sought and received permission to do an independent study in tenth grade in lieu of one of her courses. She chose to focus on the history, evolution, application, and impact of science fiction as a literary genre, advancing her theory that Mary Shelley's *Frankenstein* was the first work of modern science fiction. The end project of her independent study was authoring a science fiction short story. Her work was well received.

Chloe is very creative, and high school provided several opportunities to do some wonderful art projects. She had amassed an extensive comic book collection and created a dress with bow tie, suspenders, and full-length hoop skirt made entirely of comics. She modeled it the evening students showcased their creations. Embroidery, needlepoint, and crochet; woodworking; refinishing and refurbishing reclaimed furniture; building furniture from scratch; creating watercolor pieces that look like stained glass—her imagination is never idle.

Chloe is also a gifted writer, creating stories, poetry and keeping journals since she was a kid. I remember on many occasions reading her work and wishing I had her talent. Several pieces she submitted to young readers' magazines received awards and editors' choice recommendations.

She was successful in the process of applying to colleges and was fortunate to have several schools from which to choose. After ten minutes spent on the campus of Sarah Lawrence, the entire family knew this was the place for her. The college offers an unconventional academic and cultural experience, as compared with most American colleges and universities. Four years of encouragement and recognition of independent thought and study enabled Chloe to successfully pursue graduate work in her chosen field of history, with a concentration on the history of medicine. She completed a master's program in history at the University of Delaware, and obtained a certificate in museum studies. She is currently working in development for Planned Parenthood. We're just a little proud!

CHAPTER 27

JACK

We called him "Chicken Man." He was so skinny, we swore we could see his heart beating. And as the whitest white kid you ever saw, he was nearly translucent without a hint of color anywhere.

Jack's circumcision was a little different than Charlie's. Not done under general anesthesia (poor child) and before our very eyes (poor us). I couldn't figure out how not a single male in attendance, most especially Jay, didn't pass out. I did watch the color drain from every guy's face, like I was watching glass containers emptied of their rosy liquid.

As it turned out, the mohel who performed Jack's circumcision was the son of the mohel who was present in the OR when Charlie was circumcised. The world is the size of a marble. One farcical and ironic touch was that someone from our synagogue thought it would be nice to put flowers in the sanctuary where the bris would take place. Not just any flowers, mind you, but Hawaiian Red Anthuriums. You know—the flower with a blood-red waxy leaf and a three-inch yellow protrusion. We never found out who put those flowers in the sanctuary, but it was riotously funny seeing the look on faces as people discovered the blooms.

As we settled into life with baby Jack, exactly what we were in for was becoming increasingly and alarmingly clear, begging the question: What's the opposite of tranquil? The antithesis of serene? Whatever it is, Jack was it. Charlie was tranquil. Chloe was serene. Jack was miserable and inconsolable. And we could never figure out why he cried for as long and hard as he did. Long, like in months long. Like in really long months long. Months that felt ninety days long. No colic, no physical ailments, wasn't cold, always a clean and bone-dry diaper, well-fed, no discernible thing created his misery. But, oh my God, we often wondered how we would survive this. More to the point, how would Jack survive this? We'll have to smother him.

Maybe that's why Jay said if I wanted another kid, it would have to be with another guy.

Around nine or ten months old, Jack started to find his quiet moments. Moments of contentment, which oh-so-slowly began to stretch into hours, then days, then weeks. Our relief was existential. We thought his misery and our exhaustion would kill us off. And so did family and friends—and soon. But hallelujah! We were going to live!! Jack, too, since we decided not to drown him in the tub. He morphed into the sweetest, silliest, darlingest kid.

Right around the time he turned one, Patti and Ralph—Jack's godparents—were visiting, along with Patti's parents, Betty and Don, up from Florida. We all sat out on our deck one lovely afternoon while Betty snapped picture after picture of Jack. Don, an accomplished malaproper, mocked Betty for taking so many photos. Rolling his eyes, he looked at us and quipped, "She's a regular Cecil D. DeMille!" The incorrect middle initial was lost on Don, but not on me!

As accomplished as Don might have been with malaprops, my dad's talent not only for word misuse, but also mispronunciations blew him out of the water. To Roy, the Dominican Republic was the "Dominion Republican." Condominiums were "condominians." Detroit was "DeéTroit." The Detroit Lions were the "DeéTroit Lines." My very favorite malaprop in his repertoire was his response when I asked how he was feeling about his impending retirement. He confessed to being a little concerned that life would become too "sedimentary."

But as good as he was, a friend of my Nana's was the rightful and widely-acknowledged "Malaprop Master." Her award-winner was by way of apology when she digressed in conversation. She'd sheepishly say, "I'm sorry. I've gone off on a tandem." I believe she won the Mala-Pulitzer.

Jack had the most unusual crawling method we'd ever seen. We called it the crab crawl. I don't know that it was really even crawling. One leg was tucked under him, bent at the knee, the other straight out behind him, and he somehow pulled himself around the house in that position. It seemed anatomically impossible, but he was pretty fast.

He did give me a moment of panic when he was still on the bottle and choked on his formula. Feeding your child is blissful, whether you're nursing or bottle feeding, and I was in a bit of a trance, as was Jack. Until I looked down and saw formula coming out of his nostrils, his eyes as wide as saucers, filled with terror. I immediately sat him up and repeatedly and forcefully slapped him on the back, which started him coughing and sputtering.

That horrific feeling that I lacked the ability to keep my child safe, which I felt when battling postpartum with Charlie, came rushing into every crevice of my being—like a flood of liquid filling a large container full of sand and rocks, instantaneously filling in every space, however small. He was fine, and eventually, so was I.

All our kids were Binky eaters. From the backseat of the car, Jack loved to hurl his pacifier into the front. We felt certain he had the makings of a pitcher. He hurled those things with tremendous force. We came to keep multiple pacifiers in the car, as it was tiresome searching for them for the duration of the ride, not to mention they'd invariably land on the floor. Soon, he was simultaneously throwing two Binkies at a time, one from each hand, with equal accuracy and strength. It was crazy. And it made Jack laugh his tiny tushie off. Us too.

We proved the adage that with each successive child, parents become more laid-back. One of the examples often used to illustrate the point is that when your first kid's Binky hits the floor, you sterilize it in boiling water for five minutes before returning it to the child. With the second kid, you run it under hot water. With the third and all kids thereafter, you pick it up and wipe it against your pant leg a few times. That's pretty much how we were with Jack and his Binkies.

Jack loved to talk and started at a very early age. He'd talked incessantly and with great expression, inflection, and vocal modulation. He had so much to say about absolutely everything. The only thing was that for nearly three years, we couldn't understand a single word he said.

It was a happy development in our family when Jack's speech became intelligible. He was uproariously funny and reveled in saying outlandish things. It was the highlight of the day for whoever was within earshot when these jewels popped out. Often, none of us had a clue where they came from.

When I went into the upstairs bathroom to discover poop on the floor beside the toilet, I called Jack into the bathroom and asked if he knew anything about it. He said he tried to poop standing up. Why, you ask? (As had I.) He explained that he was afraid the Kraken from *Pirates of the Caribbean* was in the toilet and might grab him if he sat down. When I suggested that pooping while standing was tricky, vis-à-vis ensuring the poop lands in the toilet, he said, "Yeah. When I heard it *splat* instead of *splash*, I knew it hit the floor."

Many of Jack's Greatest Hits were associated with pooping and peeing. Before he started to do his own paperwork, if you know what I mean, he didn't like me checking in. He asked me not to come into the bathroom until he was ready.

"How will I know when you're ready?" I asked.

He thought for just a moment, then offered, "When the splashing stops, I'm done."

Made sense. I just had to listen very carefully.

As Jack grew, it became apparent he was a cautious, even fearful kid in certain circumstances. It was also obvious that he did not want to feel afraid or let his fears stop him from doing anything. He forged himself into one of the bravest and most courageous people I know. The trepidations started at an early age, some of which persist. And still, he is, as he was, doggedly determined to overcome them.

When he was about seven, we went cave crawling in New Hampshire. It was such a cool experience, but for Jack, more than a bit harrowing. There was a ladder bolted to the wall of one cave, which had to be negotiated to enter the very dark cavern. Jack was so frightened his entire body was trembling. He could be overheard quietly and with great determination, repeating to himself over and over, "You can do it, Jack. You can do it!" And he did.

Jack has always had a fear of heights. That's what flummoxed me when I recently saw a video of him with some colleagues in Italy, jumping off a cliff into a small pool of water some thirty feet below. I had to watch it fifteen times before being convinced it was Jack. He said it took about half an hour on that cliff to work up the courage. I have no clue how he did it. It was thrilling and nerve-wracking to watch. But I knew the satisfaction he felt in overcoming a very substantial fear.

As a kid, Jack was unable to shower without someone in the bathroom with him. Fortunately, Shirley or Mamie could be his bathroom buddy, enabling him to shower without Jay or me present. Finally, in true Jack fashion, he decided he was ready to conquer this fear but had to figure out exactly how to do it. Our nightly ritual was to lie in bed together, cuddling and chatting. On this particular evening, he wanted to strategize about what to do if something he was afraid of came into the bathroom while he was showering.

The conversation went like this. "What do I do if a monster comes in the bathroom?"

"What do you think would be effective?" I asked.

"I could throw the soap at it."

"I think that would work!" I said.

"What about a ghost?" queried Jack.

"I'm not sure. What do you think would frighten a ghost?"

"I think getting sprayed with water," opined Jack.

"Brilliant!" I said.

This went on through vampires, zombies, and werewolves. He came up with solutions for each one to include hitting the intruder with the washcloth, squirting shampoo in its eyes, and screaming at it at the top of his lungs. I knew that would work. Then came the last question.

"What about *cannibolts*? What if *cannibolts* come in the bathroom?"

"It depends on how many come in," I suggested. "How many are you afraid of?"

His answer... "One, and up."

Having the strength to refrain from rolling around in his bed in hysterics made me realize I was actually Hercules.

Unfortunately, the entire strategy disintegrated when Jack had finally decided he was able to shower with no one of any species in the bathroom. The first time he attempted it, he left the bathroom door ajar, and the escaping steam tripped the carbon monoxide detector just outside the bathroom. "Emergency! Emergency! Evacuate the premises immediately!!" Really loud. He came flying out of the bathroom and down the stairs stark naked and soaking wet. It took him six months to try again.

Jack was incredibly indulgent with Chloe, allowing her to put him in dresses, paint his nails, and basically treat him like one of her dolls. We have hysterically funny photos of Jack and his friend Daniel when they were seven, with Jack in a Snow White dress and Daniel dressed like Belle from *Beauty and the Beast*. They both looked quite fetching.

One afternoon, Jack told me he wanted to be the blue Power Ranger, so I had to find something blue to put him in. The only thing I could find was a bright blue dress that Charlie had brought from Mexico for Chloe, with a little flouncy off-the-shoulder, fringed ruffle, and brightly embroidered flowers around the bottom. But it *was* blue. Jack seemed to be perfectly content. Until I found him sitting on the stairs, looking rather forlorn. I asked if he was OK.

He answered, "I'm noohvus."

I asked what he felt "noohvus" about.

He said, "Well, look at me."

I said, "You have a point."

None of my kids take after their mother in the cursing department. I generally speak like a mob boss, but my kids could barely bring themselves to say "hell." Soon after moving to Cohasset, we enrolled Chloe and Jack in sailing lessons. We so wanted them to be into the things we most loved, sailing and skiing.

Jack came home from sailing class one afternoon, clearly irritated. I think he was eight at the time. When I asked what was troubling him, he said he was always paired with the same kid who wasn't very nice and continually told him he was an idiot because he couldn't do things properly and would insist Jack let him do everything.

This seriously pissed off Jay and me. We discussed the situation and came up with a solution, which I shared with Jack a few days later when he and I were together in the car. I told him the next time this kid called him an idiot, he had our permission to say, "Oh yeah? Well, you're a fucking asshole!"

Jack was aghast. He asked me if I was sure. I said I'd never been so sure of anything in my entire life. He said he didn't think he could say that.

I said, "OK. Let's practice. I'm going to call you an idiot."

Hesitantly, he said, "OK."

I said, "Jack, you can't do anything right! Let me do it!! You're an idiot!!"

To which Jack replied in the highest, reediest voice you ever heard, "Oh yeah? Well, you're a fucking asshole!"

I praised him to the heavens for a job well done. He said he thought he needed more practice.

More than a week went by before the next sailing class, with no opportunity for Jack to try out his new strategy. So as not to get rusty or lose confidence, he decided to practice a little more. Jay had completely forgotten about all of this when Jack went to him one afternoon and said, "Dad, call me an idiot."

A bit confused, Jay agreed to play along and said, "OK. Jack, you're an idiot."

Jack exclaimed, "Oh yeah? Well, you're a fucking asshole!"

As luck would have it, I was within earshot and spent the next half hour doubled over. And for those who might be wondering, I'm painfully sorry to tell you that Jack never did have the opportunity to exact his exquisite revenge. But I have no doubt the kid's still a fucking asshole.

Jack was in third grade when we moved to Cohasset. We decided to move in the midst of the school year so the kids could more easily make friends and have a comfortable start the next year. Being so skinny and short, and tenaciously translucent, Jack was immediately bullied.

One kid liked to come up from behind him, put his arms around Jack's midsection, and lift him up, which Jack hated. He decided not to tell us about this until the last day of school before winter break. As the kids were packing up their backpacks to head out to the buses, he saw this kid approaching and dropped to the floor. The boy kicked Jack and said, "I'll let you live until next year."

That was a bridge too far, even for Jack, and he told us what had gone on that day when he got home. Luckily, I had no access to a truck. We sprang into action, and to the great credit of the principal and counselor, they dealt with the situation beautifully. It ended, fortunately. Interestingly, the bully had enough smarts to realize if he wanted his team to win the spelling bee, he needed Jack on it. He invited Jack on the team, they won, and all was forgiven.

Jack did share one tidbit that delighted me. He told us that another kid said to him, "I'm stalking you, Jack Tillman."

To which Jack replied, "Well, if you're going to stalk me, don't you think you should know my last name?"

That's when I stopped worrying about Jack.

At six and eight, it was time to take Jack and Chloe to DisneyWorld. We'd taken Charlie at seven, and at seventeen, he felt he was a little too old for the experience. What looked to be a fairly tame roller coaster called Big Thunder Mountain Railroad seemed like a good choice for our first ride. There were no steep climbs or drops and it appeared to be reasonably horizontal. Jay was in the first car with Jack. That was our second mistake. Choosing this ride was our first.

He was too short to easily reach the bar we knew he'd cling to for dear life and was practically bent in half. Soon after the ride began and picked up a bit of speed, he looked back at me in the car behind with the most hilarious expression I'd ever seen on his face—a combination of terror, fury, and stupefaction. Outraged, he asked a slightly different version of the question Charlie asked, sitting in that darkened movie theater in Florida, watching Huck Finn's father chase him with a cleaver. Jack's was, "Mom, what made you think I'd enjoy this??" He managed to get through it without having a stroke, but it did cement his mindset for the remainder of the trip.

Jack was now in full-tilt, cautious-bordering-on-scared-out-of-his-little-wits mode but desperately wanting to have fun. He figured if he could be prepared by knowing every single detail about every freaking ride, he could decide whether to risk his life, as if he were an engineer assessing the structural integrity and failsafe mechanisms of each and the likelihood of being ejected in mid-air and crashing to his death.

And now came the questions. The incessant, relentless, unceasing questions. How fast does this one go, and how high does that one go, and is that one in the dark the whole time or just at the beginning, and does this one land in the water and if so, does it go underwater, and if not, how does it keep from going underwater and if it doesn't go underwater does it splash very much and if it does, how much water comes into the ride? Will I drown?

This went on throughout the entire trip. Jay and I put together a schedule on our second day that we followed religiously, determining how long each of us would shepherd Jack before handing him off to the other. Jay's threshold was thirty minutes. Mine was five.

Jack had a beautiful voice and loved to sing when he was young. We enrolled him in summer camp at the American Boychoir School in Princeton, a world-renowned choir school. Impressed with his voice, they invited him to audition to become a student. He was accepted and offered enrollment, which we were all quite thrilled about. But when we learned they would only take him as a boarder instead of a day-student, we decided, along with Jack, that this was not for him. He was only seven! I wasn't sending my kid to boarding school at seven, even if it was in the same town!

The next summer, and for four consecutive years, Jack attended a Jewish sleepaway camp that he loved. Chloe attended for two years. I was seriously conflicted about sending the kids off to camp for two weeks that first summer. The day after they left, I was wondering who the hell ever came up with this bullshit summer camp idea, and what on earth made us think it was a good one?? I thought I'd never get through two weeks without the kids, and great discomfort settled in.

Three days later, I realized it was the wisest parenting decision we'd ever made and spent the remainder of the two weeks in blissful quietude and relaxation. It was a world-class vacation, which we intended to repeat every summer until the kids graduated college.

After the second summer, when it was time to register for the following year, with my fingers crossed behind my back, I asked if they wanted to go for four weeks instead of two. Chloe informed us she was not going back to camp. I said, "What? I'm sorry... what did you say??" She repeated her statement. I said of course you're going to camp. She said, "I'm not." I said you loved it. She said I hated it. I said you never mentioned that. She said you never asked. I said you're going to camp. She said I'm not. I said we'll pay you. She said you don't have enough money. End of discussion.

Jack played Little League and was quite excited but very apprehensive about his first at-bat, certain he'd get hit by a pitch. We explained that it rarely happens. Once again, Jack took his fear with him and did the thing he was most afraid of—and was hit in the thigh with the first pitch.

The expression on his face as he looked at his parents was similar to the one I saw on Big Thunder Mountain Railroad. To his great credit, he continued with Little League, playing on the Orioles and winning the championship. As baseball fate would have it, Jack interned for the actual Orioles his first summer after college!

Jack had a wonderful circle of friends and seemed to sail through middle and high school. We celebrated his bar mitzvah, where he did a wonderful job, and we threw a fantastic out-of-the-box party for him at a local sports complex. Everyone, including Jack, had a blast. He became a leader in the youth group at our temple and served as president, creating a mission statement and constitution to govern activities that had never been developed before.

Then, in the blink of an eye, he was a junior in high school. As we had done with Charlie and Chloe, we told Jack it was time to sit down with the *Fiske Guide to Colleges* and get a sense of the schools he was interested in. He disappeared into his room and came back with a notebook and a list of forty schools, all but ten of which were crossed out.

Jack had developed a fascination with sports at a very early age, and for a time he thought he wanted to play, but eventually focused his interest elsewhere. He invented all kinds of tournaments with his friends, which he organized in hyper-minute detail. He ran fantasy leagues with multiple players year after year. Still does.

We would not have been surprised if Jack wanted to enter the sports arena in some professional capacity. We were, however, shocked to discover that, without saying a word, he had done exhaustive research and made a list of schools that offered programs in sports journalism. He also found out who the points of contact were in the admissions department at each school and had emailed all of them.

Also unbeknownst to us, he had attended a college fair at school, interviewing reps from each school, asking his list of prepared questions. Based on his online research and conversations at the fair, he eliminated thirty of the forty schools on his list. He also announced that of the ten remaining schools, there was only one he wanted to attend: West Virginia University.

Being a good Northeastern elitist, I asked Jack what on Earth West Virginia had to offer and why he would possibly consider going there. He strongly expressed his desire to tour, and I, of course, said yes. I took him for the first college tours that included Duquesne, Marshall, Penn State, and WVU.

Neither Duquesne nor Marshall wowed either of us. WVU was next. I was skeptical stepping foot on campus, but by the time our tour ended, I was blown away by their personnel, resources, and the opportunities they could offer Jack. I said, "Well, you're going here, Jack, if I have to do something illegal to make it happen. (I guess I was ahead of my time.) We also decided when the tour ended that there was no need to look at Penn State, as WVU was a safety school where he felt confident he'd be accepted. We strategized that should there be a rejection, he'd still have time to apply to other schools.

Jack was accepted to WVU's highly-regarded school of journalism within a week of submitting his application. After his first semester, he decided sports journalism was not for him. As a rabid political animal, taking after his mother, he switched his major to political science, but even with a passion for politics, soon discovered this was not the world he wanted to enter, either. Fortunately, the school of journalism had just added a brand new major, Sports and Adventure Media, an absolutely perfect fit for him, so he happily returned to the department.

Landing a job with the athletics department, he discovered his love of and talent for video and photography. He landed three internships over the next three years: the Baltimore Orioles, the Air Force football program, and Harvard's athletic department. Upon graduation, he was hired by a company to produce videos for the sports teams at Purdue. Wanting to return to the East Coast after a year in Indiana, he landed a position as manager of creative video at Brown University, producing videos for their thirty-plus sports teams for social media. He's self-taught and, as it happens, a brilliant videographer.

With our three kids now well-established, engaged in creative and fulfilling work well-suited to their passions and talents, and either married or in serious relationships with wonderful partners and plans to marry, Jay and I have little to do in the parenting department beyond loving, supporting, and praising our kids to the heavens and anyone who will listen, whether they like it or not.

CHAPTER 28
MR. RIGHT

I know for a fact that many women have googled "untraceable poison" as they contemplated killing me off so they could grab Jay. How do I know this? Because that's exactly what I would've done if he were married to somebody else. Let's just say that when I kick the bucket, the Bundt Cake Brigade will be instantaneously lined up at the door.

While I have learned the fine art of calibrating my insanity, and can pass for a stable, reasonable, and functional woman, I spend an inordinate amount of time on the ledge and the ceiling. Thankfully, Jay can talk me in from the former and scrape me off of the latter. Were it not for him, I'd have long ago resembled Hannibal Lecter being wheeled in on a dolly in a straitjacket and goalie mask.

Between the logistical nightmare of creating Charlie's custody schedule every year for fifteen flipping years; the stress of infertility, and the gargantuan effort required to gather our gaggle; then to raise said gaggle, for God's sake; on top of caring for aging and dying parents and the day-to-day pressures of *life*, with Jay's unfailing support, I managed to ward off the breakdown.

And he brought some of life's greatest joys to me that I might have never known. A life on the water in our little cherished sailboat, The Izzy, whose namesake loved sailing more than life. And were it not for Jay, I would have never known the exhilarating thrill of skiing.

And speaking of skiing, I should give you the highlights. I didn't learn to ski until I was fifty, but never learned to stop. Stopping is a valuable skill for a skier. Crashing into a man who, at his peril, stopped on the slope; an unfortunate mishap with a ski pole tearing my rotator cuff; and a full-speed-ahead crashing encounter with the stanchion of the chairlift, resulting in broken ribs, caused me to hang up my boots, at Jay's gentle insistence, at sixty. Skiing was the most spectacular sensation and even the pain of considerable and repeated injury didn't mitigate my sorrow at giving it up.

Of course, no person or marriage is perfect. One area of disconnect for us is confrontation. I need to confront, process, and resolve challenges in all facets of life whenever possible. It's how I manage and come to grips with the world. Jay, on the other hand, will do anything to avoid conflict. I think it comes from the WASP culture. It also stems from experiencing the family-shattering devastation of his parents' divorce when he was ten, his beloved, idolized, hero dad moving out of the house, and the resulting challenges facing the family in the ensuing years.

It's a tough dynamic in our marriage—the "Grand Confronter" and the guy built to avoid conflict, otherwise known as the "Zen Master." But in the grand scheme, we are exceedingly fortunate. And, of course, it's not all luck. Jay has learned how to accommodate, compromise, and let go. I'm trying.

I like to think that I brought things to Jay's life that he might have otherwise missed: an abiding fascination with politics, a sense of adventure, a willingness to take chances, a reverence for and exploration of the natural world, and a fierce determination to see as much of the globe as possible.

Jay has taught me to be more tuned into and aware of what I can and cannot control. He's helped me see and determine my real priorities. In many circumstances, he has helped me know that calm is closer than it appears.

We're a very good fit.

Jay has told me throughout our life together that I take his breath away. Every birthday card, every anniversary card, every Mother's Day card, every note accompanying flowers contains those words. And I have vowed to love him to the end of my days with one word uttered at every opportunity... *always*.

CHAPTER 29
THE DAD DÉNOUEMENT

One of the very best outcomes in my life story is the wonderful resolution to my dad's and my troubled and difficult relationship. I wish I could tell you what brought it about, but I can't be certain. He did mellow with age, and his life was long. We said goodbye to him at ninety-eight. But my best guess is that the end of day-to-day parenting, with us all permanently living on our own, slowly gave him the room to relax in his home and no longer feel the desperate need to control what was utterly uncontrollable.

Additionally, I think that as financial strains and professional pressures began to ease, his capacity to appreciate the good fortune in his life increased. He simply became a happier man, able to allow himself to feel gratification and hopefully take pride in the life he built. He and my mom had a wonderful retirement in Florida, which they enjoyed for many years.

My dad was so happy to eventually become a grandfather and thrilled to have the opportunity to spend a great deal of time with Gershon's boys as they grew up, since they lived in Pittsburgh. And he delighted in seeing the grandkids that lived further away. My dad was in infinitely greater control of his temper as a grandpa than as a father, which made grandparenting a much less stressful and more enjoyable undertaking than parenting. He was also a fairly young grandfather, so he had plenty of energy and good health to enjoy in the role. All his grandkids have warm and loving memories of him.

As for me, especially wonderful was his expression later in my life of love and respect, and even pride in what he saw as my talents, accomplishments and abilities. To hear, and more importantly feel, admiration and approval from him meant the absolute world to me, softening the jagged edges and barbs of the pain that lingered for many years.

But of it all, perhaps the most striking revelation was coming to the realization, as I parented my own kids, that massive amounts of patience, even-handedness, strength, restraint, rationality, calm, and saintliness are needed at nearly every freaking moment of each freaking day.

And there you have it.

When my life ends, as now, I will have nothing but abiding love in my heart for my sweet and sentimental dad.

CHAPTER 30
ONE FROM EACH COLUMN

I ran into my friend, Helane, in Princeton when I was pregnant with Jack and told her my happy news. After receiving her heartfelt congratulations, accompanied by lots of hugs and kisses, I shared that I would soon have a genetic kid, an adopted kid, and a kid born from a donor egg.

She said, "Wow! That's amazing!! You should write a book!! You could call it *One From Each Column*!" I thought that was a fabulous idea and a compelling title. I'm going to do that! I'm a decent writer and have something to offer in my story. I'm definitely going to do that!! It could really be helpful to people. People who are trying to build their family through alternative methods. I have a unique perspective that could shed light and uplift. I'm absolutely going to do it!

That was twenty-six years ago. I tend to procrastinate.

But procrastination can create opportunity. My kids are grown, and I'm writing what will likely be my first and last book. Procrastination in this endeavor gave me the great gift of perspective and a driving motivation to put it all down.

So, here's what I know—and I know it because I lived it. Parenting is a fusion of actions, thoughts, fears, worry, hopes, goals, desires, intentions, responsibilities, disappointments, and dreams. Thousands of dissimilar moments all at once and one at a time. Realizations. Confusion. Under-standing.

While pregnancy is wondrous, it does not make us parents. If a preg-nancy is carried to term and culminates in a birth, it makes a mother or a father. Not a parent. Parenting is in the doing.

My mother was with me when Charlie was a newborn as I changed my first diapers. She stood next to me as I gagged over one that was particu-larly grotesque, causing me to breathe through my mouth. Chatting while changing, my mom could hear I was holding my nose and said, "Honey. This is your son."

I replied, "Mom. This is shit. Hideous shit."

Changing a diaper like that without puking all over your baby is parenting. Sitting up all night with your kid as he cries inconsolably is parenting. The first kiss from your child, the first hug, the first word, the first step, the first peals of laughter, the first ice cream, broccoli, injury, nightmare, the first day of school, the first playdate, the first team tryout, the first bike, the first lie, defiance, mischief, obstinance, punishment, song, dance, drawing, day of camp, puppy love, puppy heartbreak, driver's license, car accident, prom, formal dress, tuxedo, the first application to college, the first rejection, the first acceptance, the first day, the first job application, job interview, the first offer, *ad infinitum...* is parenting. I could fill another book with the million pieces of parenting. And it's all learned on the job with quite the curve.

A FEW LAST THOUGHTS

Whenever we take on a weighty challenge requiring a difficult decision, we identify and unpack the problem; develop the goals; determine the best options for achieving our objective; do our best to ascertain the potential pitfalls; decide whether or not to embark upon the journey; and if we choose to go forward, work our damnedest to ignore the irrelevant and unimportant concerns beyond our control. We keep our eyes on the prize, our head high, and we power through based on our well-placed sense of confidence.

In nearly all things of consequence in life, when a decision is made, the components of that decision will almost always include a leap of faith. Whatever form our faith may take, we do well to rely upon it in life's often unknowable circumstances. And we ultimately come back to the adage of the ages: shit happens. But most often, it doesn't.

In modern times, many options exist, making it possible for the greatest dream in the lives of so many to come true: the dream of becoming a parent and having a family. As I look back on all the challenges and obstacles in my path since childhood, I know that when options exist, so do aspirations and the promise of fulfillment. And there are always options.

Two of our three children would never have come into our lives were it not for the existence of various courses of action. With a keen understanding of the challenges, the tremendous difficulty and pain posed by infertility, and profound appreciation for the treatments and alternate methods enabling us to create our family, Jay and I were so happy to make ourselves available to speak with individuals and on panels about our experience. I'd like to share with you what we so gratifyingly shared back then with those in the throes of infertility, borne of our experience and triumph.

Many assume and fear that they will not be able to perceive a non-genetic child as their "own," rendering them incapable of bonding with and loving that child as they assume they would have had the baby been born to them "naturally." Men seem to face this challenge more often and deeply than women, sometimes unable to overcome their doubt and misgivings. Men often are most challenged around adoption or kids born from a sperm donor, afraid they'll feel as if they are raising "someone else's kid."

I hope our experience can quiet and even put to rest many of these worries and anxieties.

I am a big believer in and advocate for transparency. I have known families who have chosen to keep the truth hidden from their adopted, surrogate, or donor children. There are many reasons that such a decision is made, but, in my opinion, it never serves the well-being or best interests of the child or family. Keeping secrets is rarely a good thing, especially when kept from those we most love.

With both Chloe and Jack, we openly talked about their origins from the first moments of their lives. Talking about Andrea and where Chloe came from and how we found her and why we wanted her and how fortunate we were to be her parents started from our very first day with her.

We spoke with Jack about Laura, his donor, and how we found her, and why we went that route, and what he meant to us, his genetic connection to his father, and his biological connection to me. We talked about all these things from Day One. (Jack is not my genetic child, but he is my biological child since he gestated inside me.) We read books to them, watched videos together, and helped them own their origin stories and take agency from them.

Also fascinating and important to know is that adopted and donor kids often feel very differently with respect to how much they want to know about their birth parents and/or donors. I know of kids who, from an early age, wanted to know everything they could possibly know about their birth parents or donors, and even had an interest in meeting them if it was possible to arrange.

Neither Chloe nor Jack fell into that category as they were growing up. As I said earlier, Chloe did develop an interest and found her birth family through social media a few years ago. Jack never had any interest beyond knowing what is in his donor's profile and feels no differently now. He knows that if he ever developed a desire to learn more or to possibly meet Laura, we would do everything in our power to make that happen.

A great way to approach it all is to follow your kid's lead. They'll make their feelings, desires, and comfort level known, all of which should be appreciated and respected. A good rule of thumb... offer, don't push.

Lastly, remember that support and social groups abound. These can be wonderful ways to manage whatever challenges you may face and to create connections for your adopted and/or donor children with others like them. When Chloe was in nursery school, we discovered that several children in her class were adopted. We excitedly organized regular get-togethers with the other adoptive families. We became good and close friends, and it was a beautiful thing. Some of those relationships remain to this day.

I'd like to offer some guiding principles we gathered along the path...

ON GETTING A KID THROUGH DIVORCE WITH MINIMAL DAMAGE

I learned a few things during the painful and difficult experience of my divorce, which I'd like to share with you. It is my great hope that these insights will never be useful to you.

Somehow, I instinctively knew that establishing and committing to a predictable structure—providing consistency and reliability in Charlie's residential schedule—was crucial for his activities, schooling, socialization, and more. Ironically, a key part of making it all work was flexibility.

Our greatest chance of success in getting Charlie through this divorce with as little damage and baggage as possible, was the degree of cooperation, civility, amicability, and shared goals Dean and I could identify and achieve right from the start. Sadly, there was considerable bitterness between us, hindering our ability to accomplish this on as regular a basis as I hoped for. And saddest of all was that Charlie had to swim in those waters for many years. It broke my heart.

- The most meaningful measure of a successful divorce is the mental health and emotional well-being of the child. If you get that right, you're light-years ahead of the game. After all, marriage can be finite. But when kids are involved, divorce is forever. If parents are motivated to destroy their ex and inflict as much pain and misery as humanly possible, that's exactly what they'll mete out to their children, with exponential effect. The burdens they bear, especially those imposed by their parents, will ripple through their lives, perhaps indefinitely.

- A child has no means by which to manage these burdens. Unless they're emancipated with financial resources, they have no option to seek out therapy. At a younger age, a child will likely not even realize they're experiencing trauma or have the ability to identify what they're feeling. They just know they're unhappy, maybe afraid and worried, wondering if it's their fault, thinking what must have been their bad behavior is to blame. That's an unwieldy weight for a child to bear. They have no frame of reference to understand what's happening to them. They wouldn't know to seek out an adult to talk with or may not know anyone they'd want to talk to. Unless their parents choose to have them see a therapist, which could be enormously helpful, they are simply not at a stage where they can seek or summon support in navigating these waters. They're often left to sink or swim.

- As a divorcing or divorced parent, one of the most important things you can do for your kid is let them know you support them in their love of and desire to spend time with their other parent. Remember that your child's love for your ex in no way diminishes their love for you, ever. In fact, quite the opposite can happen. Your child's love for you can be deepened, strengthened, and enhanced in knowing that you fully support them in their love for their other parent.

- And always, with what will sometimes require a super-heroic effort, take the high road. The parent seen as mean, vindictive, resentful, blaming, and punishing is the parent who will suffer. Let's put it this way: Your ex can be an asshole, but if your kid perceives that you think so, especially if you treat them as such, or portray them to your child as such, in their eyes, you're the asshole. A child is drawn to and protective of the parent whom they perceive to be the weaker one. And they can find it nearly impossible to forgive the parent they see as the perpetrator.

- If you are in the unfortunate situation where your partner or ex is speaking ill of you, whether deliberately or inadvertently, there is little to nothing that can be done to stop them from doing so. It would require communication so the issue can be processed between the parties. When that's not possible, you must maintain your faith that your child will come to understand eventually what impact that behavior might have had on their opinions of and feelings for you. Children of all ages possess a deep and powerful sense of fairness, and their feelings about their parents will, in part, be based on whether or not they deem them to be fair people through this difficult situation.

- Do not foist upon your child your opinions of your ex. Their transgressions, mistakes, weaknesses, inadequacies, etc., in whatever form they may have taken, do not need to be known by your children, at least not coming from you. Do not look to your child to be a therapist, confidant, ally, or friend. They deserve and need to be protected from their parents' blame, vitriol, or bitterness. There's nothing they can do about any of it, nor should they be asked to.

- Additionally, the burden of divorce is hefty enough without adding to the weight of responsibility they'll invariably feel for maintaining the peace and making their parents happy. That is not their job. And you need to help them know that.

- Professionals can be enormously helpful to you and your ex-partner, as well as your child. Family therapists, psychologists, mediators, clergy, and social workers are all available to work with parents, together and/or separately, and can involve the child when appropriate and useful. If the other parent agrees, therapy for just the child can be arranged, and the therapist may include the parent/s from time to time. If your partner/ex is unwilling to work with professionals, that shouldn't preclude you from seeking out their advice and guidance. These resources can be found online, through friends, family, clergy, or a local community center. I cannot stress enough the value of this assistance. It can be a game-changer not just for your child, but for you, providing immediate, mid- and long-term relief.

- Lastly, one of the greatest tools a child can have, enabling them to live an independent, functional, fully actualized life of good mental and physical health, is a sense of personal power, whether their parents are in a happy, successful marriage, or get divorced.

We empower our children when we listen to and really hear what they have to say. By demonstrating that we want to know their feelings, opinions, ideas, fears, worries, desires, preferences, etc., and acting upon what we learn whenever possible, they feel seen, heard, and respected. This is how we confer a sense of power, agency, and control, making it much less necessary for them to seek out those things in other, often less healthy ways. In so doing, we impart independence, self-confidence, value, and self-worth. There are no greater gifts we can bestow as parents.

ON ADOPTION

Our adoption experience was complex and multifaceted. I'd like to share with you some of what we learned and insights we gleaned in the hopes that you might find it helpful should you ever consider adoption.

- Perhaps knowing what we went through with Chloe has struck fear deep in the heart of those in the throes of infertility, contemplating adoption, and perhaps causing you to consider abandoning the option altogether. It's important to know that the great majority of adoptions are successfully finalized without any issues or concerns about revoked consent or other challenges. I would not want anyone to think that what happened to us happens with frequency. It does not.

- Also, adoption can take several forms. "Open" adoption has become more commonplace than in the past, offering birth families the opportunity to be a part of the child's life in one way or another, to varying degrees, depending on the preferences and goals of the birth and adoptive families.

- Because we believed it would be best for Chloe, we were committed to establishing an open adoption so her birth family and we could have a good deal of interaction and engagement, dictated by feasibility and the level of comfort of all involved.

- "Closed" adoptions, where there is no engagement whatsoever between birth families and adoptive families, were practiced more often decades ago and are still chosen under certain circumstances. Conversations with social workers, adoption specialists, clergy, friends, and family can help an individual or couple determine their goals for their adopted child and their family, their comfort levels, and which arrangement would be best.

- International adoption, once very popular in the U.S., has seen a sharp decline due to a significant decrease in the availability of internationally adoptable minors.

- Another significant statistical change is that today, more than forty percent of adoptions are transracial. This is up from twenty-eight percent in 2004. Several challenges have been identified for children adopted transracially, including coping with being different from their immediate and extended family, struggling to develop a positive racial/ethnic identity, and an ability to cope with discrimination and bias.

- Parents adopting transracially should do everything in their power to educate themselves, their entire immediate and extended family, and their child about their racial identity, culture, heritage, and traditions, and celebrate that heritage. Raising awareness amongst their children's teachers and educators, friends and friends' families, their religious and social communities, as well, is very important. Also critically important is creating opportunities for the child and family to engage with people and communities who share their racial background. They must be tuned into and vigilant about their child's well-being living in a transracial family and perhaps a community offering less diversity than they might like.

- Some fear there will be physical, medical, or mental health challenges with an adopted child, or issues arising from conditions of their origins, or horrible things occurring that can never be anticipated or known. Those "this wouldn't have happened if we'd had our 'own kid'" scenarios. And for some, the fear is overwhelming. It stops them dead in their tracks.

- What many fail to consider is that scenarios of all kinds can arise in any circumstance. A fully biological/genetic child born to an individual or couple can encounter all the same potential issues and challenges that might befall an adopted child. We often operate from the false assumption that we know or would know everything that can be known by way of medical and genetic history with our "natural" children, and to a certain extent, that's accurate.

- But there can be earlier history we cannot be aware of, and even recent history that, for any one of a number of reasons, is outside our scope of awareness and understanding. It is simply not possible to anticipate everything. Random occurrences happen that have nothing whatsoever to do with medical history or genetics. This, of course, can be the case in any child brought into our lives by any method.

- When these fears and concerns arise, we are best served by remembering that the vast majority of children born, however, their conception and birth may occur, are born perfectly well and will, in all likelihood, live a life in good physical, mental, and emotional health.

- Some folks obsess over what others—family, friends, neighbors, and colleagues—"will think." They internalize embarrassment and even shame, worrying if and how they'll be judged on all manner of issues arising from their infertility and decision to adopt. In my experience, the opinions of those who would feel entitled to judge, especially in this realm, hold no value, worth, or consequence. With those whose opinions do matter, open, candid, and ongoing conversations can be especially helpful to address concerns and misconceptions, answer questions, and generally engage around adoption and why it was chosen as the best option to build a family.

- And, of course, it is the right of every person or couple considering adoption to remain private about their decision and process. No one is entitled to any information except that which is offered freely. Here again, conversations with and support of professionals, clergy, and trusted family and friends can be extremely helpful.

ON GOING THE DONOR-EGG ROUTE

Here are several important things to know about using a donor. There are myriad scenarios when utilization of donor sperm, eggs, or embryos would be seen as the best option to accomplish a pregnancy.

- According to UCSF Health, single women or lesbian couples will often use a sperm donor to accomplish a pregnancy. Male factor infertility is a common reason for a couple to choose donated sperm. Cancer, hormonal disorders, sexual dysfunction, obstruction, or an injury to reproductive organs can all be reasons for the use of donated sperm. Couples may seek a sperm donor to avoid passing on a genetic disease or disorder that is carried by the male partner. In other cases, sperm donation may simply be the best option due to conditions affecting sperm count or motility. Perhaps there's a complete absence of sperm, or simply that prior treatments using the partner's sperm have been unsuccessful.

- UCSF Health goes on to say that egg donation is often an excellent option when age is the issue, negatively affecting the health and viability of one's eggs. Perhaps early menopause, premature ovarian failure, diminished ovarian reserves, genetic diseases, repeated IVF failure, or a history of cancer treatment that damaged one's ovaries will prompt the decision to choose egg donation.

- There are countless resources available that can, with the help of a professional to guide the process, support people in identifying and choosing a donor who would be considered a match, according to a set of criteria and objectives established by the individual or couple. Just like with adoption, the donor and recipient can decide if they're open to or interested in any contact, and if so, how much and under what circumstances.

- People often wonder what motivates someone to become a sperm or egg donor. Recent years have seen a dramatic increase in individuals choosing to become donors, and their reasons for doing so vary. There can simply be a financial incentive. Donors are financially compensated, and that income is used in various ways. And fees can vary widely. Many individuals have put themselves through college by donating multiple times. Others simply benefit from the fee they will collect for one donation.

- Some people will donate primarily out of a sense of altruism and the desire to help individuals and couples build families who otherwise might not be able to. Sperm and egg donors are sometimes parents themselves and want others to experience the joy they have in their own lives. Still, others may donate to leave a genetic legacy. Perhaps they do not plan on becoming parents but want to contribute to the growth of future generations. Others may see donation as a way to promote reproductive freedom, helping individuals and couples overcome biological barriers to parenthood.

- The process of donating sperm is simple and easy (and, of course, enjoyable!). Donating eggs, however, is not simple or easy. It requires a considerable amount of time, the injection of multiple medications, and a somewhat invasive procedure for eggs to be harvested and fertilized for transplantation.

- All of the above reasoning for egg or sperm donation can apply to a decision to choose embryo donation. Additionally, embryo donation is easier now than ever before. With better technology, greater awareness, and more structured programs, embryo donation is now a more viable and widely accepted option for those seeking to build their families. The process can be smoother, success rates can be higher, and there can be more choices available to match intended parents with the right embryos for them. Embryo donation has become a more accessible and streamlined option for family building due to advancements in medical technology, growing awareness, and the expansion of embryo donation programs.

- Donors will indicate whether they have an interest in meeting a child born of their donation. The recipient family may decide from the outset whether they would like to have some degree of engagement and would choose a donor accordingly.

- As with adoption, an open-minded approach to donation is more common than in the past. There is less stigma and controversy attached to the practice of sperm, egg, and embryo donation, and more comfort in choosing what's best for each party.

- Nevertheless, there are still those who would disagree with the practice for some personal reason and perhaps negatively judge a person or couple who decides to use donation as a means to build a family. And of course, they are entitled to their opinion. Likewise, those who choose donation are entitled to dismiss their judgment.

I spoke earlier about the universal and often confounding questions facing so many in the grip of infertility. Questions to which many feel desperate for answers. Can I love and bond with children to whom I did not give birth as I would with "natural" children? Can they love and bond with one another and me in the same way?

And so I leave you with the most important message of all, the one I've so passionately hoped to impart in this book.

The most compelling proof I can offer to illustrate the total absence of difference in loving and bonding with the children we bring into our families through alternative methods is this...

Forty-seven years since The Decision, thirty-seven years after Charlie was born, twenty-eight years after Chloe came along, and twenty-six years since Jack's arrival is the continually mind-blowing fact that I still forget that Chloe was adopted and Jack was born from a donor egg. I find myself wondering from time to time if I had morning sickness with Chloe or only Charlie and Jack. Was she as active in utero as Jack? Was I as exhausted in my first trimester with Chloe as I was with Charlie?

I long ago lost sight of the fact that Jack is not my genetic child. Jack more closely resembles me in temperament and passions than Charlie, my beloved and "naturally conceived" firstborn. Chloe in her utter uniqueness and dissimilarities is no less my child and is fully of me. The nature of the love and bond between all three kids and Jay and myself is the same. Exactly the same. And the love they each feel and demonstrate for us and one another is identical.

What I want you to know is simply this... it does not matter how our children come to us. Only that they come. The rest is hard work, delight, determination, fear, joy, worry, satisfaction, wonder, luck, hope, and so much more. And the deepest love you'll ever know.

EPILOGUE

I am not a person of faith. I often wish I was and could look to, believe in, pray to, and rely upon some theological entity. While I am an observant Jew, I do not ascribe to a belief in Adonai, at least not in the way religious Jews do. Many of the people I most admire, respect, and trust in this world are believers, and I long to understand the nature of their belief. I've often thought about hosting a series of theological salons where ideas and ideals of faith can be explored, shared, and possibly, for me, explained. But with a master's in procrastination, my salon series never materialized. Of course, I'm not dead yet, so there's time.

I do believe, however, that certain forces are very much at play in the universe—love, kindness, compassion, beauty, mercy, justice, and truth. This unstructured and disorganized belief system constitutes my definition of God. I am also an ardent believer in the reverent sanctity, majesty, and immense power of the natural world. It is nature in all its glorious manifestations upon which my spirituality is based.

Otherwise, my faith consists of optimism and hope, tenets deeply and forever embedded in my DNA. In great part, they comprise my M.O. in all things. Not to say they have not been greatly challenged, even fundamentally shaken at points throughout my life. They certainly have. But they've never abandoned ship.

Perhaps these attributes created the lifelong stamina needed to rage against the forces seeking to shape and control my life. Don't tell me "no." I will not stop until I unearth, manufacture, or conjure the "yes."

Infertility, the biggest "no" the universe handed me, gripped me and flooded me with fears and primal misgivings I had never encountered before. Not much in life is as devastating and demoralizing as infertility. Long-standing dreams, expectations, and assumptions of what life would look like are thwarted—crushing hopes, breaking hearts, often inflicting crippling self-doubt and sometimes shame. I spent six years battling those forces.

But even in the darkest moments, a tiny flame of hope and optimism burned in me. The Little Pilot Light That Could, even if dimly at times, illuminated the path and guided my steps. That light was lit long ago as six-year-old Fightin' Little Jodi squeezed herself into a ball under the dining room hutch and resolved to be furious rather than fearful. From six to forty-six, when the last check was gleefully entered in the final column, it was that often dim little light that led me all the way home to my magnificent family.

And so it is with deep gratitude that I wish you, my dearest reader—from the very bottom of my heart and every nook and cranny of my soul—only and all good things as you traverse whatever challenging landscape you may be trekking. If I have provided a sense of promise, hope, and optimism, I will rest well knowing that the telling of my story served its purpose and fulfilled my mission.

I leave you with many thanks and much, much love.

WITH GRATITUDE

Thank you so much for reading my book. I'm truly grateful for your time and interest, and I so hope you enjoyed it!

To learn more about the services I provide, based on my personal experience overcoming trauma and navigating infertility, please visit my website. You can learn about my keynote speaking, my dynamic online course, *From Powerless to Parenthood and Points Beyond*, and my guest appearances on podcasts and panels. To book me to speak at a virtual or live event, or to guest on your podcast or panel, kindly visit the Keynote Speaking page on my website.

On my Resources and Free Gifts page, you'll find various free offerings I'd be thrilled to share with you. I sincerely hope what you discover there brings you clarity, value, and promise.

Kindly scan the QR Code to visit my website,
and I'll be happy to meet you there!

www.ingramcontent.com/pod-product-compliance
Lightning Source LLC
Chambersburg PA
CBHW031518120626
46545CB00005B/1911